A FOREWORD FROM THE PRO

One of the great things about our game of golf is that it's the same for all of us. Golf is a game of skill that puts into play our own personal challenges and helps us overcome them.

Golf is often said to be a metaphor for life. It teaches us many things about life, such as

- Ethics and personal honor
- Appreciation for the self, others, and Mother Nature
- Enjoyment of contests and personal challenges
- Cooperation can be an integral part of competition

Of all our great golf champions, one man relished the personal challenge inherent in golf more than anyone else. That man was William Ben Hogan. Hogan realized that overcoming his own obstacles to success through golf made him a better player – and a better man.

In this book, you'll feel as though you are looking over Hogan's shoulder as he faces his personal challenges. You'll discover that Hogan in many ways is just like you – with challenges to face, decisions to make, and chances to take.

You'll also discover Hogan's formula for success and his fabled secret of golf. Hogan arrived at his formula for success after a lifetime of trials. It's a formula you can apply to your life right now to achieve success in golf – and in life.

I hope you like this book as much as I did. I wish you an enjoyable game of golf and a great life.

Golfingly yours,
Nate Gumm
Membership Direcor

Trophy Club Country Club
500 Trophy Club Drive
Trophy Club, Texas 76262
817-837-1900

Also by Bob Thomas:

Golf Gave Me Something to Love

Why Bobby Jones Quit

The Old Man and His Game

The Old Man and His Golf Book

BEN HOGAN'S SECRET

A LITERARY PORTRAIT

Bob Thomas

Email the author: Hoganbook@aol.com

Published by:
Bob Thomas Books, Inc.
PO Box 853
Black Mountain, NC 28711

First editon published by:
MACMILLAN
A Simon & Schuster Macmillan Company
1633 Broadway
New York, NY 10019-6785

Distributed by:
Bob Thomas Books, Inc.
PO Box 853
Black Mountain, NC 28711

Cover design by Robert Bunch

Library of Congress Cataloging-in-Publication Data is available upon request.

ISBN 0971768226

Printed in the United States of America

CONTENTS

A Note from the Author vii

Acknowledgments xi

Chapter 1
The Hogan No One Knows 1

Chapter 2
What the Sportswriters Never Discovered About Hogan's Past 21

Chapter 3
The Fates of Bobby Jones and Ben Hogan Are Linked Forever 37

Chapter 4
The Magic of a Repetitive Swing 53

Chapter 5
Hogan Discovers His Biggest Handicap 73

Chapter 6
Jones Meets a Kindred Soul in Hogan 83

Chapter 7
The Sportswriters Almost Ruin Hogan's Game 105

Chapter 8
Hogan Gets Even 121

Chapter 9
The Shadow Emerges 131

Chapter 10
Hogan Becomes the First Comeback Kid 157

Chapter 11
The Ultimate Secret of Golf 181

Chapter 12
The Real Hogan Emerges 201

A NOTE FROM THE AUTHOR

I grew up with Ben Hogan. Not with the man himself, but with stories about him. Details of his extraordinary life and his enormous love for golf settled somewhere inside me and never left me alone.

While other kids discovered the new medium of television, I lugged golf bags up and down the hills of a Donald Ross course. My first year as a caddy was Ben Hogan's banner year in professional golf: 1953. That year, Hogan did what no other professional has done before or since. He won three modern major golf tournaments.

Hogan's achievements thrilled me to the bone that year, and I dreamed a young man's dream of becoming a great man, just like my hero, Ben Hogan. It was not to be for me, but it was and always will be for Ben Hogan.

As I grew older, I began to hear unfavorable stories about my hero. In one of them, Gary Player went to Hogan for help with his game and Hogan turned him down. I was shocked. This was not the Hogan I knew. The truth emerged later. Gary Player had indeed gone to visit Hogan, seeking his help, and Hogan had graciously accommodated him.

I heard other stories as well. Some painted Hogan as a money-chasing miser, others as a nasty grump. Those who knew him, however, mentioned his generosity, his shyness, his devotion to his wife and to the game of golf. This latter

Hogan was the Hogan I grew up with, the man who challenged himself and me to find my passion.

Some say Hogan deserved the rumors for being a recluse and for not taking the time to correct misstatements. But, that's not how I saw it.

Yes, he was a recluse. He didn't want the acclaim everyone heaped upon him. He just wanted to play golf, to compete, to win, to challenge himself – and it made perfect sense to me. Isn't that why we all play the game of golf? To challenge ourselves? To find our passion and let others find theirs?

In *Ben Hogan's Secret*, I wanted to examine those questions by depicting what it might be like to be Ben Hogan. To do that, I faced a severe handicap. There are many books written about golf's champions, but very few written about Ben Hogan, and none of them an authorized biography. He was, very simply, a private man.

Therefore, this book is a literary portrait. The details, dialogue, thoughts, letters, motivations, and spiritual meaning as well as Hogan's ultimate secret are my interpretation and come strictly from my imagination. Yet this book is based upon the facts of Hogan's life. For example, it is known that Hogan was invited to the 1938 Masters by Bobby Jones and that his invitation was a surprise. It is also known that he played a practice round with Jones. However, their conversation as recounted in this book grew from my imagination.

I didn't write this book to please Ben Hogan, although I was hoping that it would. If it pleased him, it was the first printed account of his life that did.

I wrote this book for you, the reader, to tell you about a man I came to love, who stands for something this world needs. I wrote this book as I felt it, and I let the story come to me.

It is the story of what can be done with a life. It's the story of an unfailing commitment to excellence, of the rewards that go with using the strength of the human spirit to its fullest.

In many ways, the story ended up in a different spot than I had envisioned. At first, I thought I was looking for a mechanical secret, for no account of Hogan's life would be complete without discussing his fabled secret of golf. But the more I looked at his life; the more I felt I had a bigger secret on my hands. A man who came from nowhere, who went through a war that interrupted his game in its prime, and who lived through a crushing accident to become one of golf's greatest players, didn't have a secret as light as a mechanical shill.

Instead, I looked for the secret in his life – in the last place anyone has looked for it. As Grantland Rice, one of America's most revered and talented sportswriters so aptly put it, "His legs weren't strong enough to carry his heart around." That was Hogan. Transferring his love for golf into my own game, and into my own life, has enriched me beyond words. If it enriches yours, I have done my job well.

This book is an effort to give us all another look at Ben Hogan, and I would enjoy hearing your thoughts. Please feel free to drop me a line.

Bob Thomas
Hoganbook@aol.com
June 1, 1996

ACKNOWLEDGMENTS

To Don Horak,
a man who carries the spirit of the game
from the course into his daily life.

My thanks to Ben and Valerie Hogan for living such an inspiring story.

My wife Mary Anne contributed greatly to this work, as she has to my life.

Without the help of Don Horak, this book would not have been. A special thanks, Don.

Following the trail of those who helped in one way or another: In Pinehurst, North Carolina, Mary Rose Busby, Neva Sherry, Walt Braxton, Jr., J. Peter Stokes, Randy and Kathy Burchfield, Brig. Gen. Roberts (Ret.), and former Governor Jim Holshouser.

In New York, Brian Fradet. A special appreciation award to you, Brian, for all your support.

In Raleigh, North Carolina, Carl Tharin, Jack Coats, and Jackie Murdock. Thank you, Jackie, for being the man who returned Hogan's one-iron to him.

In Salem, Oregon, Dave R. Chapman. Find me an error now, Dave.

In Savannah, Georgia, Ron Hansen, Ernie Hannah, Tommy Schaff, and two real Southern gentlemen, Mr. Albert Stoddard and Mr. Lefty Waters.

In my exciting new field of publishing, I have a few people to thank for many reasons: Brian Lewis, Patty

Leasure, Tom Grady, Mike Leonard, Ken Brown, Steve Quinn, Rick Wolff, Guthrie Kraut, Gary Ink, and Egon Dumler.

A special thanks to Traci Cothran for being my first and acquiring editor, and of course to my current editor, John Michel, for his enthusiasm and hard work, and to my publisher, Natalie Chapman, who believed in me.

Let's do it again.

Chapter 1

THE HOGAN NO ONE KNOWS

BEN HOGAN HAD A SECRET, and in the spring of 1996, when he was eighty-three years old, he wanted to keep it that way. A secret.

The handful of people who knew him well understood why. They knew it would reveal more of Ben Hogan than Ben Hogan wanted to reveal. The rest of the world, who knew only what the sportswriters wanted them to know, thought he was a curmudgeon who selfishly kept his secrets to himself.

Rumors of a secret had dogged Ben since his astonishing comeback from a near-fatal automobile accident in 1949. As the injured pro made his remarkable return to the sport, a notion began to take hold: A man who can barely walk but can win golf tournament after golf tournament must have a secret.

Ben hated the public discussion about a secret. He was a private man and painfully shy. He winced when fans and sportswriters dissected his physical movements, his decisions, his life. He found comfort in routine and control, and rumors of a secret were the one thing Ben could not control about his life. Consequently, the rumors became the soft spot in his carefully erected veneer, the chink in the Hogan armor.

In 1955, Ben relented to public pressure and authorized Life magazine to reveal his secret. He labored over a multi-page spread explaining a trained movement of the wrist, which he called "pronation," that eliminated the possibility of a hook. It was the most scientific article about golf that had ever appeared, and Ben looked forward to the end of the rumors.

To his utter dismay, the article only fueled more speculation: A man who knew so much about golf must have more than a technical secret to share. No one believed that Ben had revealed his real secret.

They were right. His real secret was too raw, too private, too powerful to divulge.

Ben was almost ready to talk in 1992. Golf Digest was notified that Ben Hogan himself had decided to divulge his secret. Golf Digest dispatched a reporter to Fort Worth only to learn that Ben demanded a six-figure price. The magazine declined, and as suddenly as the urge to reveal his secret had come upon Ben, it passed.

Then, on a warm, late-April day in 1996, following the Masters Tournament, fate intervened in Ben Hogan's life once again, and the one thing he couldn't control came tumbling out.

The sun was bright and clear that day as Ben shuffled through the kitchen of his Fort Worth home and out to the garage. With typical Hogan precision, he scanned his vehicle to make sure it was ready to go. Those who knew him understood that it was because of his near-crippling accident. Before the accident, Ben had been a careful driver. Now, he scrutinized every aspect of vehicle operation before he even got in.

As he pulled out of his driveway, Ben quickly assessed the weather. It was warm today, almost too warm, and he wondered if he should switch to his summer schedule. He was still on his winter routine: breakfast at a roadside diner, mornings at his ceremonial office at the Hogan Company's Fort Worth plant, and afternoons on the golf course at Shady Oaks, where the warm sun boosted the circulation in his permanently stiff legs.

Ben made a mental note to switch to his summer routine the next day, May 1: golf in the mornings when the sun was still warm but before humidity made things unbearable. It was the same decision he had made at the end of April for nearly twenty-five years now.

As he pulled into the parking lot of his favorite roadside diner, he made note of the time on his dashboard and saw that he was early. He smiled when he saw that his Cadillac was only the second car to pull into the lot. He would be served quickly and without interruption. It was a small detail, the kind most people ignored, but it was second nature to a man who had spent most of his life training himself to notice the slightest change of grip, swing, or stance.

Ben dropped two quarters into the newspaper box outside the restaurant and pulled out a *Dallas Morning Herald*. As he sat down at his favorite table near the window, not far from the kitchen door, he turned to the sports page.

"Mornin', Mr. Hogan," his waitress said. "The usual?"

"Mornin', Theresa. Yes, in cream, thanks."

As she poured his coffee, Ben thought back to the years spent on the road when he'd been unable to get the Texas-style food he craved. He had promised himself that once he got off tour, he would always eat his favorite foods – like eggs cooked in cream.

"Thank you," he murmured as she finished pouring. It was the same modest, soft-spoken acknowledgment he had offered to fans as they cheered his shot – so soft that most didn't even know he had made it.

As usual, Ben didn't linger over breakfast and headed back to the car as soon as he had finished. When he arrived at work, he wasn't surprised to find that his secretary of twenty-three years had arrived there before him. Glancing at his name on the company logo as he entered the building, a personal sense of achievement came over him.

"Good morning, Mr. Hogan," Mrs. Hilliard greeted him brightly as he opened his office door.

"Mrs. Hilliard." He suppressed a shy smile. His days were predictable now, but he never lost the feeling of delight at seeing the same people and doing the same things week after week, year after year.

"Is the mail here yet?" he asked.

"Yes, it's on your desk and sorted. There's a letter on top that I think you'll want to have a look at."

"What about that new promotional photo?" he asked.

"Right here," she said and handed him a glossy black-and-white photograph.

Ben regarded it quietly. On the left was an image of his swing in the early fifties at the peak of his career. On the right was a shot of his swing in the late seventies. "Some great things never change," the copy read, and even Ben smiled at the effusive praise.

"Very good," he said softly and handed back the photo.

At his desk he automatically reached for the pile of mail on the right, the children's letters. Even though he had been off the pro golf tour for over twenty-five years, Ben still received a great deal of mail – everything from business propositions to requests for interviews to fan mail. The letters he liked most of all came from kids. Ben had no children of his own, yet despite this, or perhaps because of it, he had a soft spot for youngsters.

Ben began to read the first letter on the children's pile, and he understood why his secretary had thought he would be interested in it. It was carefully written in pencil on lined notebook paper.

> Dear Mr. Hogan,
>
> My name is Billy Watson. I play golf every day here at Tampa Bay Hotel Golf Course. I really like the game a lot and hope I can be as good as you someday. Some of the guys said you own a golf club company. I am writing to see if you can get me a good deal on some new clubs. The ones I'm playing with are falling apart. With better clubs, I know I can play better. I'm a caddy, and I have some money saved to pay for them. If you can give me a good deal, I won't have to wait any longer.

Ben thought for a moment and then opened the bottom drawer of his desk. He pulled out a directory of PGA professionals, paged through it until he found the Tampa Bay

Hotel Golf Course, picked up his phone, and dialed.

"Pro shop," a voice answered.

"Tim Struthers, please. This is Ben Hogan calling."

Ben heard a muffled voice in the background. "Hey Tim," the voice called out, "Ben Hogan's on the phone for you." Laughter. "Yeah, that's what he said."

Tim Struthers picked up the phone. "Yessir, Mr. Hogan," he said with a joking tone in his voice. "What can I do for you?"

"This is Ben Hogan of the Hogan Company in Fort Worth. I received a request from a young boy who caddies for you," Ben began in an unemotional, businesslike voice. "His name is Billy Watson. Are you familiar with him?"

Hogan's no-nonsense tone and his mention of one of the caddies by name convinced the pro that he was indeed talking to the famous Ben Hogan. Struthers began to stutter in response. "Y-Y-Yes, Mr. Hogan. As a matter of fact I do know Billy."

"What I'd like is –"

"Billy's a good kid, Mr. Hogan." Struthers's words nervously tumbled out and interrupted the legend on the other end of the line.

"Well from his letter –" Ben said, trying to continue.

But the pro quickly interrupted again, embarrassed at his babbling but unable to stop, "Every now and then, you meet a young boy with promise, someone who works for everything they get without squabbling. That's Billy."

As Struthers took a quick breath, Ben wasted no time explaining the purpose of his call. "He asked me for a good deal on a set of matched clubs. He told me he had almost enough money saved."

"Billy comes from a family of six children. They don't have much money, and he gives part of his caddying money to his family. It's unlike Billy to go outside his family for anything, Mr. Hogan. I'm –"

This time Ben interrupted. "What I'd like you to do," he instructed, "is measure Billy for clubs and call my secretary with the details. With the next order you place, I'll throw in Billy's clubs as a promotion. Pass some of the savings on to Billy and you'll both come out ahead."

"T-T-That's very kind of you, Mr. Hogan. I'll be sure to let Billy know what you've done for him."

"No," Ben said, an edge creeping into his voice. "I don't want you to let Billy know about our deal."

"I don't understand."

"Just consider it part of my secret," Ben said, chuckling as he put the phone back on its cradle. Comments about the secret always create silence, Ben thought.

It took Ben nearly an hour to go through the children's mail. For some, he autographed pictures; for others, he wrote encouraging notes or pulled a birthday card from his desk and signed it with a flourish, always adding his favorite saying: Golfingly yours.

He looked at the pile of letters on his left with a sigh. Business letters – his least favorite. He had no way of knowing that this stack held the key to his future.

Ben pulled the pile to the center of his desk, hoping to run quickly through them and head out to the golf course, when a small note from his secretary caught his eye. It said, in her familiar hand, *Package from L. Wadkins in the corner of office*.

The message momentarily stunned Ben. A package

from Lanny, he thought. Why would he be sending me a package?

Spotting a long tube in the corner of his office, Ben walked over to it. "Probably a new promotional poster Lanny wants to show off," he chuckled. He popped open the top and saw a long, thin item, sturdily wrapped as though it secured something heavy. It was not a poster.

Surprised, Ben tilted the tube and a note fell onto the floor. Picking up the paper, Ben realized it was attached to a separate envelope. He read the note first.

Dear Ben,

A fellow I went to Wake Forest with asked me to forward this to you, and I am sending it along per his request.

Best wishes,
Lanny

Ben then opened the envelope and extracted a letter addressed to Lanny from his former classmate:

Dear Lanny,

I found the enclosed club at a golf collectors swap meet. It's an unusual golf club, dating from 1948 or '49. There weren't many one-irons back then with such a stiff shaft. It's also worn precisely where the "sweet spot" is and has a custom-made, thick grip.

Could this be the one-iron Hogan lost after the 1950 Open

at Merion? I am sending it to you in the hopes that you can get it to him. If it's Ben's, tell him it's back where it belongs.

Ben was slightly dazed as he opened the package. The man who sent the club had done a careful packing job. It was wrapped better than any club Ben had ever seen, with plastic woven around the shaft and club head, covered by strong packing tape.

His hands shook as he reached for the small, old Barlow pocket knife he kept in his desk drawer. Could this really be my old club? He thought, and his mind wandered back to the 18th hole at Philadelphia's Merion Country Club. He frequently remembered that particular shot, the one that had won him the 1950 U.S. Open, but rarely had the memory been this strong. It was almost as if he was back at Merion.

Ben recalled his feeling of relief right after completing his approach shot to the green on the long par-four. He had needed a par on that hole to get into a playoff with Mangrum and Fazio. With the hole measuring 458 yards and a slight breeze in his face, he had counted on his one-iron to get him safely onto the green with his second shot. The club had done its job. Then it had mysteriously disappeared from his bag.

Now, as he unwrapped the package, he saw that it did indeed contain an old MacGregor Hogan one-iron. As he continued to cut the wrapping off with his knife, he was still at Merion and could feel the two-club breeze stroking his left cheek.

Ben pulled off the last of the wrapping and finally gripped the club. It felt good in his hands. He addressed an imaginary ball and, waggling the club, said to himself, "No doubt about it. I've had this baby in my hands before."

Sitting down in his office chair as if to have a talk with an old friend, Ben gripped the club and tapped the club head on his shoe just as he had done years ago.

He remembered the talks he had had with the club, believing it would help them understand each other. Maybe the talking really did help, he thought, as he recalled the glory the difficult-to-hit one-iron had brought him.

"What should I do with it?" he wondered aloud, and then quickly answered the question himself. "I should give it away for display." But overcome by nostalgia, Ben realized he did not want to let it go so soon.

"Oh, don't be a sentimental old fool," he quickly chided himself. And remembering a recent request from the USGA museum for more memorabilia, he prodded himself some more, "Just give it to Golf House!" Meanwhile, his old friend rested against his knee, listening to every word.

"I could give it to Colonial," he thought. But he quickly ruled them out, since they already held his main display of trophies and awards.

"Yes, I think you should go to Golf House," he decided, addressing the club, "since you were lost during the play of a U.S. Open." As an afterthought, as if seeking the club's approval, he asked, "Okay, old friend?"

Ben wrote a note to Mrs. Hilliard. *Send a note to Golf House and tell them I am donating the one-iron that was used to hit the approach shot to the 18th hole at Merion in the 1950 Open. Remind them that this shot was featured in* Life *magazine.*

He started to replace the club in the tube and suddenly realized he would never see it again. Stopping, he took the club back out and looked at it very closely. He had used it so many times he had worn a little spot about the size of a dime on the face of the club.

Ben gazed at the spot intently. Then he held the grip of the club with his thumb and a finger of his left hand. Starting at the toe and proceeding toward the heel, he tapped the face of the club head with his finger in order to determine the "sweet spot" of the club.

The sweet spot, he discovered, was precisely where the face on the old club had been worn down. He smiled with the confirmation that he had been getting the most out of the club all those years. Pleased with his own perfection, he recalled the last time he used it.

No one ever knew what had happened to this one-iron, which disappeared after the fourth round of the 1950 U.S. Open. For years, rumors circulated that it had been stolen; it was, after all, the club responsible for his victory.

In fact, Ben had removed a seven-iron from his bag to comply with the USGA rule of allowing only fourteen clubs and instead had substituted his one-iron. Before the tournament started, he had determined how he would play each shot on each hole of the Merion course. He was so methodical that he knew in advance there were no shots that would require a seven-iron.

It would be nice to practice with this one-iron again, he thought. I wonder if the old magic is still there. Ben left a postscript for Mrs. Hilliard, *I'll bring the club back tomorrow morning for shipment*, and he headed for Shady Oaks Country Club.

Ben was uncharacteristically off schedule as he pulled into the club's parking lot. He parked as usual, backing in and pressing the automatic trunk button. A caddy would be expecting Ben's arrival and would put his regular clubs and any new test clubs onto the golf cart. Ben headed into the dining room for his second cup of coffee before starting his private practice session.

In practice Ben needed solitude. It allowed him to concentrate on what he was trying to achieve, rather than on spectators who wanted to study him to learn his secrets. The members and staff at Shady Oaks knew this and had learned to respect his privacy.

Ben had originally practiced at Colonial Country Club in Fort Worth, where his trophy room was located. After Shady Oaks was built, however, he had switched his practice sessions to this new club and now used a secluded area off the side of one of the par-fours, where he could practice almost unobserved.

This morning, even though he was late, the waitstaff in the dining room had protected his favored seat, which overlooked the 9th and 18th greens.

His waitress was waiting for him to arrive. "Good morning, Mr. Hogan. Great day to be hitting balls, isn't it?" She had no way of knowing her casual comment would turn out to be so prophetic.

"Good morning, Martha," Ben replied. "Yes, it's a beautiful day to be hitting balls."

"The usual, or plus rye toast?" Martha asked, referring to Ben's habit of ordering coffee plus rye bread toast to give him extra energy for practice.

"All the way, the works," Ben said with a grin, letting her know he needed the energy today, of all days, for a special practice session. As the waitress left, Ben remembered the times on tour when he would have enjoyed a cup of coffee with his toast but had bypassed it to make sure his hands were steady for putting.

The one-iron had not yet left his side. It rested against Ben's left leg, a subtle reminder of the majesty that was once his.

Ben picked up the newspaper the waitstaff had carefully placed on his table. It was another copy of the *Dallas Morning Herald*, and Ben again pulled out the sports section. He found a sports column summing up popular reactions to Greg Norman's spectacular loss of the 1996 Masters. Ben wondered why the article had missed his attention earlier.

"I know what Norman needs," he suddenly realized, "and it's not what everyone is talking about."

In a strangely reflective mood, Ben swirled his coffee as he remembered his own second-place finishes, before he had discovered the secret. He grimaced when he saw the similarities between his pain and Norman's.

"It's not going to help him to be bathed in sympathy for losing. Sure he feels good now, but it will set him back, and he won't even know why."

The waitress interrupted Ben's thoughts again, this time with his breakfast in hand. He ate a little more hurriedly than usual, anxious to get to the course and feel the swing of the one-iron. After signing the tab, he headed out the door past the pro shop to his waiting cart. Ben checked the cart to make sure nothing had been overlooked: golf shoes, a thermos filled with iced tea, his current favorite clubs, and a few new iron designs from the Hogan Company. In his back pocket was the little black book he always carried to mark the results of his latest practice session.

Driving the cart with his one-iron beside him, Ben nodded and smiled at the familiar faces he passed. Arriving at his practice area, he tried to force his mind back into his routine. He inspected his tee box to make sure the grounds crew had filled and seeded his previous divots; he then methodically placed his shoes and thermos on the padded bench installed especially for him. He surveyed the scene for a moment, as though honoring the precision that had led to his enormous skill.

Ben waved to his caddy, who was waiting for him in the middle of the field. He still enjoyed the tradition of the game, the prestige of having a caddy retrieve his golf balls. Over the years, Ben had perfected a system of hand signals to tell the caddy where to locate himself as a target, and such was his accuracy that no caddy had ever been hit.

Striding back to the cart to choose a club, Ben stretched to get his body ready. Since the accident he was always somewhat stiff, never completely limber.

Then, holding his eight-iron, Ben signaled the caddy to step backwards and slightly left. He dropped his hand to signify his approval, and the caddy adopted a shortstop pose to prepare himself for the arrival of Ben's first shot.

Ben's pattern was to hit three draws of twenty feet, three fades of ten feet, three low straight shots, and three high straight shots. After each shot, he wiped the club head and analyzed the shot. He especially checked the trajectory to see how well he had performed his swing routine. Then, he moved the next ball from the pile of balls on his left and placed it beside the spot from which he had hit the last ball.

After finishing a few more stretches, Ben began to

punch out his first practice shots. Ben was accustomed to hitting good shots, but for some inexplicable reason, on this day all his shots went exactly where he wanted them to go. Even his warm-up shots were perfect.

Each eight-iron landed within inches of the caddy. Occasionally, one of the balls actually hit the pile of balls the caddy had created in front of him.

Feeling how sharp his game was, Ben now took out his two-iron and motioned the caddy to move straight back until he was about two hundred yards out. Allowing for the fractional right-to-left wind he had noticed, Ben stroked the ball. It came to rest within a few inches of the caddy. He tried another shot and got the same result. The third shot hit the pile of balls at the caddy's feet.

Ben was pleased, then disturbed. As he hit shot after shot with each of his irons, progressing through his bag from his two-iron to his sand wedge, he realized this practice session would rank as one of the best he had ever had in his long career. Shot after shot after shot landed exactly where it was intended to land.

Even though he paced himself, Ben found he was winded from excitement and sat down on the bench to rest. While resting, he marked his results in his black book, savoring each good stroke as it came back to him.

He wrote down 12 for 12 with the eight-iron, 12 for 12 with the two-iron, 12 for 12 with the five-iron, and the same for every club he had pulled out of his bag. Each shot precisely on the mark. It was incredible.

Buoyed by his results, Ben thought, I'll try my four-iron punch shot. Let's see if I can do as well with one of my problem children.

As he swung his shortened grip firmly and crisply through the ball, Ben knew what the result would be. It was as if the result had been telegraphed to his brain by the feeling flowing through his arms, across his shoulders, and into his neck. The four-iron shots were the best he could hit, not more than twenty-five feet high, landing, and running straight for the target.

Remembrances of other punched four-irons flooded over him. At Pinehurst in 1951 with Henry Longhurst, fans were enthralled with his shot on the 17th hole. At Carnoustie in 1953, the wind picked up during the second round, and he exchanged glances with Bernard Darwin, a now-elderly British golf writer who, after the match, had said, "I thank God for allowing me to live long enough to see Ben play this round."

I wonder what Darwin would say if he saw today's practice round? Ben thought.

Another memory came back just as quickly. At Augusta in 1967, his score of 30 on the back nine included a punched four-iron on the 11th hole to keep it below the wind. The shot had been a rare occurrence for him. Because the pond on the 11th hole at Augusta had been expanded to include a steep slope, Ben never went for the green on his second shot. That day he did, and it was a beauty, rolling to within five feet of the cup and giving him a short putt for a birdie.

The hair quivered on Ben's arms as he relived the shot. He wondered why the rush of memories was so strong. Must be tied in with the great practice session, he thought. But why now, why today?

Ben's excitement quickly turned to confusion. He liked

living in the present. His motto was, "Yesterday's gone, that's why they report it in the newspaper."

Maybe these remembrances come with age, he thought. But what about the fantastic practice session he had just marked in his book? Did that come with age, too?

Ben refocused his thoughts on the last club in his bag, his old one-iron. He had last hit with it on June 11, 1950. Reaching for it now, Ben felt the hairs on his arms stand up again and a chill run down his spine. Taking the club in his hands, he observed it closely and grinned again when he saw the little worn spot.

He coaxed a ball into place with the head of the club and addressed it, feeling a thrill of anticipation course through his body. He waved the caddy back to the 220-yard mark, his maximum distance for a one-iron. He was feeling very gutsy.

His first shot with the club was a long, low draw that swung out to the right, then back to the left, as it zeroed in on its target. It hit fifteen yards short of the caddy but rolled the last few feet to finish at the caddy's feet. His second shot was a repeat of the first, again rolling to the caddy's feet.

Ben decided to try a high draw, the kind that was repeatable only after years of practice. As he swung, he aimed to hit the ball farther out on the face, toward the toe of the club, slightly higher than the sweet spot. The shot took off almost twice as high as his previous shots and again drew back to the left, finishing up at the caddy's feet. His face lit up with the unparalleled joy of a perfectly executed shot. "Boy, that felt good," he said to himself.

His fades with the old club left nothing on the tee.

Taking off to the left of the target, they hung in the afternoon sky and gently glided to the right and to their target. He didn't know who was enjoying the shots more, he or the one-iron.

Ben finished his practice session with three high shots and three low shots that were more like rifle blasts, as shot after shot expertly and effortlessly hit its mark. Putting the one-iron in his bag, Ben smiled warmly and was overcome with the feeling that, in some way, the club had always been with him.

As he pulled up to the clubhouse in his golf cart, he was in such deep thought he missed nodding to a couple of members. It was as though they hadn't even been there. He was suddenly acting just the way he did when he was on tour.

"Just accept the fact that you can now hit 168 shots to land exactly where you want them to land," he said to himself. Then he laughed, realizing the idea was absurd. True, but absurd. He laughed again, more like a snort, remembering that even in his dreams his best round of golf was nineteen shots for eighteen holes. In that dream, he had missed the 18th hole when the ball rimmed the cup and spun off. "Damn, I'll still have to make one putt," he had said when he woke up.

Leaving the cart, he shuffled to his Cadillac and started the engine without checking the car for the first time in many years. He headed for home still trying to comprehend what had happened to him.

It was the secret. Again.

As carefully as Ben had constructed his life to avoid the ramifications of his secret, fate had intervened once again.

The reappearance of his one-iron had brought it rushing back to the forefront of his life.

As he approached his house, Ben pushed the button on his garage door opener and watched the door rise before he pulled the big car into its normal resting place. Getting out, he realized his legs felt unusually heavy and tired.

Heading into the kitchen through the side door with the one-iron still in his hands, he had to double back and close the garage door. Boy, he thought to himself, Valerie would have been shocked if she had seen that garage door open.

Ben's love for his wife was legendary, and he always shared his every thought with her. But today Valerie had gone shopping with a friend, so he would have to struggle alone with his memories.

Setting the one-iron next to his favorite reclining chair in the den, he headed for the refrigerator. Selecting two oranges, he washed and cut them in half with a sharp knife. Then he cut them in half again, finally bisecting each piece until there were sixteen triangular pieces in a cereal bowl.

"This is just like the tour again!" Ben muttered. In his early days on the tour, before his first top-ten finish allowed him a chance to keep playing, there had been a point where he and Valerie had been so poor they had only oranges to eat.

Sliding into his recliner, Ben took out his little black book and looked at his latest entries as if to reinforce the fact that the practice session had actually happened. After seven decades of golf with countless strokes and rounds, Ben found himself looking at a book that told him he had just had the ultimate practice session.

"But why now?" he asked, squirming in his easy chair.

Putting down the oranges, Ben went to the closet where he kept his little black books from past years. As he looked through one after another, more memories flooded back. He remembered the endless practice sessions at Augusta National when he was writing his first book, *Power Golf.*

"I wish Bob were here to tell me what this means."

But as quickly as this thought came to mind, another surfaced, and Ben knew he could no longer hide from the truth. Shaking his head, he realized he had known the reason for his extraordinary practice session as soon as he had picked up his old one-iron.

It was because of the secret he shared with Bobby Jones.

Chapter 2

WHAT THE SPORTSWRITERS NEVER DISCOVERED ABOUT HOGAN'S PAST

SECRETS DO NOT SPRING from champions fully grown. They are formed by time and events; their roots planted deep within the psyche, hidden from everyone's view, left to grow into sadness or greatness. For Ben Hogan, it was to be greatness, but it started with rejection.

Ben watched rejection kill his father and from then on it became a festering root at the core of his introverted psyche, a magnet that would draw heartache as well as a secret.

In the first two decades of the twentieth century, the Hogan family lived in Dublin, Texas, a small rural town sixty miles southwest of Fort Worth. Ben's father was a blacksmith, making a poor but happy living shoeing horses for nearby horse and cattle ranchers. By 1920, however, the ranches were turning into agricultural farms and didn't have much use for a blacksmith.

Instead of meeting this change with the optimism of a man who could handle a challenge, Ben's father greeted it with the defeated air of a man who had been cruelly rejected. And Ben, his older brother Royal, his sister Princess, and his mother watched Chester Hogan succumb to a deep despair beyond their rescue.

When Ben was ten years old, the final chapter of his father's life came to a hideous close.

"What was it like, Royal?" Ben later asked his older brother. "I mean, did Dad say goodbye to you?"

Royal Hogan did not answer right away; his thoughts involuntarily returned to the loneliness of that cold February day.

After an unsuccessful day spent wandering the streets for work, Chester Hogan had returned to their small rented house. Coughing and hacking from a winter cold, he pulled his .38 caliber pistol from its hiding place in the bedroom closet and rested it on his lap.

Royal heard the slight noise and looked for his father, finding him in the bedroom. He rushed forward, hoping to hear good news.

"Father, what are you doing?"

Chester Hogan lifted the gun, cast sad eyes upon his oldest son, and pointed the barrel just above his heart.

Royal screamed as his father pulled the trigger.

When Ben asked about the last few minutes of his father's life, Royal answered only with a blank, icy stare. It was as if part of Royal's spirit had fled at the same moment as his father's.

Years later, long after Ben had become a fixture on the pro golf tour, sportswriters jokingly called him "the ice man" because of his steely resolve. Every time they did, however, Ben remembered Royal's stare and relived the pain of his father's suicide.

Friends who had known Ben both before and after his father's death felt the tragedy had driven the young Hogan's personality inward. At age ten, never a child and already a man, Ben faced both pain and responsibility with a new head-down, eyes-ahead, forward walk. It was the stance that would be captured in some of golf's most famous photographs in years to come.

Ben and his brother, Royal, went to work and Ben's first job was as a newspaper boy selling papers to the incoming and outgoing passengers at the Fort Worth Railway Station. Because the job required him to be up early each morning and work until late each night, on more than a few occasions he was found asleep on the station benches.

Watching his brother struggle to uphold responsibilities that might have defeated even grown men, Royal searched for jobs that would be easier for Ben. One day, he heard a group of boys talking about carrying golf clubs at the Glen Garden Country Club.

"Boy," they said, "you should see how much those guys

make carrying bags. It's a lot more than hawking newspapers." Those words were all Royal and Ben needed to hear.

The following morning found Ben at Glen Garden before anyone else arrived, having hitchhiked and walked five miles in the dirty, dark morning hours to get there. He had already made up his mind. He would become a caddy and bring home more money for his family than any other caddy.

But before Ben could turn this idea into reality, he had to overcome a few problems. The rejection that would haunt his entire life came into play for the second time.

The older caddies did not want Ben to join their ranks. It wasn't personal. They just didn't want to share their good-paying work with a new boy. Most caddy applicants went away when a welcoming committee of older caddies, made up of the toughest-looking boys, said, "Sorry kid, the ranks are closed."

Ben Hogan, however, took a little more persuading.

"Hey, don't you get it, kid? You're not welcome here."

Ben did not move. He clenched his jaw and thought about the money he could bring home to his mother.

"Didn't you hear?" another caddy shouted. "We're not gonna share our loops with you."

Ben looked toward the first tee, where groups of golfers would soon be gathered.

Several of the boys rustled nervously, wondering what to do about this new boy, when one of them shouted, "Gauntlet!"

The older caddies sprang into action, quickly lining up in a double file and creating a crude pathway toward the pro shop where the caddies reported for work.

The jeering started.

"Scaredy-cat!"

"See if you want to stay now!"

"You're a chicken and your old man is, too." They had no way of knowing Ben's father had just committed suicide.

It was an awful jab but just the thing to motivate Ben. An icy stare came over Ben's face, and he began to run through the ranks to the pro shop.

As he did, the boys pummeled him, yelling at him to go away. It was difficult to tell which was worse for Ben, the rejection or the beating. Hard fists struck his shoulders and his back. A foot came from nowhere and knocked him to the ground.

Ben stumbled to the end of the gauntlet and turned to face his accusers. Singling out the oldest caddy, a boy who weighed at least forty pounds more than himself, Ben drew back his fist and punched. The two boys fell to the ground in a tangle of angry fists.

No one intervened and Ben did not stop until the other boy was curled into a ball, protecting his face from unrelenting blows. Finally, Ben stopped, rose to his knees, and then to his feet. Quietly, he brushed the dirt from his pants and headed toward the pro shop.

The crowd was hushed for a minute, until one boy about Ben's size stepped forward and asked, "What's your name, kid?"

"Ben Hogan."

Ben walked into the pro shop and registered as a caddy. No one stopped him.

On that day golf became a symbol of mastering life's mysteries for Ben. He learned that what nature did not provide, sheer will did.

From his first day as a caddy, Ben brought good money home to his mother and family. It wasn't just ordinary money; it was money earned from his first victory. Ben's thrill at helping his family, his pride in making a difference, cemented him to golf and began his lifelong love affair with the game. He would never forget that golf had enabled him to become a man.

In later years, as his life was coming to a close, Ben was heard to say, "I feel sorry for rich kids now. I really do, because they're never going to have the opportunity I had. I know tough things. I had a tough life, and I can handle tough things. They can't."

Ben's self-esteem was now entwined with making as much money from golf as he possibly could. When it rained, he hawked golf balls, looking for almost-perfect lost balls called "pearls" that he resold for a good price. He picked up a few broken-down, abandoned clubs at Glen Garden, and he watched the members as they practiced, hoping to learn how to play the game. Caddying was one thing; playing was another. As a golfer, he could get a steady job as a club professional.

Practicing golf shots became a sanctuary to him. When he practiced, the world left him alone. No one called him names, no one reminded him his family was poor, and no one told him he had no future. He was left alone with his dreams of making money from golf.

Soon, Ben's only positive feelings about himself emerged when he was practicing golf shots. Consequently, his schoolwork suffered. It was time to make a decision that would embarrass him for the rest of his life.

"Ben," Royal had said, "what are you going to do about school? You haven't been there in over a month."

"I don't need schooling to be a golfer, Royal. I can make more money for Momma out here on the course."

"You'll make Momma happier by getting your diploma," Royal said. "She has her heart set on one of us finishing high school, and you like learning better than I do."

"I'd rather make her happy by seeing that she has a roof over her head and food to eat," Ben snapped.

"You're only fourteen!" Royal answered. "You don't have to be the man of the family yet. You can go to school in the mornings, caddy in the afternoons and on weekends."

"But I'll make more money being here all day," Ben argued, not wanting to give up his only safe place in life.

"Please, Royal," he said softly, "don't you and Momma take that away from me."

Ben Hogan became a high school dropout, a registered failure. Now, he had no choice but to put his game together. Some of his early moves benefited his game; some hurt it. For years, sportswriters attempted to discover the origins of Ben's infamous hook, the one that would keep him from winning tournaments as a young pro. They had no idea it was created during his caddy days.

According to the rules of the caddy yard, the caddy that hit the shortest drives had to pick up all the balls. Because Ben didn't want to waste time, he was, of course, determined to hit the longest drives. Within a short time, Ben learned that a ball hit with a right to left draw went farther than a ball hit with a left to right fade. The only problem with Ben's draw, however, was that it was a hairsbreadth away from a deadly hook. And so, Ben Hogan, three decades away from being the world's greatest golfing champion, purposefully drilled into his memory a draw – and a hook – so that he could earn a few more pennies each day.

All of Ben's early technical lessons, including his draw, were learned on discarded or badly worn clubs, one of them a left-handed five-iron. Monday mornings, the slowest day at the course, usually found him peering over a barrel at the local hardware store, carefully choosing used clubs for a dollar. Most of them were not really playable; their hickory shafts were warped and their club heads were rusted.

"Hickories" by nature couldn't hold up to the requirements of heavy and constant hitting. It wasn't very difficult to break the hosel rivet or even the hickory shaft itself, and therefore practicing shots was an oddity for most golfers, amateurs and pros alike. Practice would only speed the inevitable damage to the hickory and replacing a shaft was a costly and tedious job. So Ben's bargain barrel clubs gave him an edge over other golfers – then, when he was young and years later, when he had become a champion.

With his cheap clubs, Ben was able to practice hard, and it was a good thing he did because he could not rely solely on the natural talent other young champions-to-be had, like Byron Nelson, his rival for the annual Glen Garden caddy tournament.

In 1928, the tournament was traditionally held the day after Christmas, an opulent holiday for the members of the club but only a dressed-up celebration of bare essentials for families like the Hogans.

This Christmas, however, Royal had another idea. A few weeks before Christmas, he interrupted his mother, who was at the kitchen table counting the money they had saved and worrying about how to stretch it through the holidays.

"Momma, I know what we can buy Ben for Christmas," Royal said.

"That's nice, Royal," she replied, hardly looking up from her calculations. "I hope we'll have enough money to buy a nice Christmas dinner for a change this year."

"But, Momma," Ben's sister, Princess, interrupted. "Royal has a great idea for a present for Ben."

"Well, what is it?" Clara Hogan said abruptly, now that her attention had been wrenched away from the practicalities that governed her existence.

"Ben's been saving his money to buy that new set of golf clubs at the hardware store," Royal said. "He needs a good set of clubs to be a golfer, and there's only one set left with Christmas comin' on. If someone else gets it, Ben's only chance will be gone."

"Ben works so hard for all of us, Momma," Princess butted in, "he deserves those clubs."

"How much do these golf clubs cost?" Clara asked, knowing that it was an impossible dream but longing to dream a little, too.

"Thirty-five dollars."

"Thirty-five dollars! How do you children think we'll ever get that much together? And for golf clubs no less." Clara sunk her head down into her hands.

"I've got forty-five cents to contribute, Mom," Princess said quietly, wanting to do her share like Ben and Royal.

Clara paused, looking at the young girl's eager face, not wanting to disappoint any of her children but knowing that disappointment ruled their days and their dreams.

She sat quietly for a moment, and neither child dared interrupt. Clara thought of all the things she wanted to give her children, the clothes, the bicycles, the good food. She also knew that as she deliberated Ben was probably lugging golf clubs around the course for sixty cents a round. What would he want her to do?

As Clara Hogan looked into Princess's eyes, she saw the light of generosity shining brightly there and realized that her daughter's eagerness to help Ben was more important than anything she might buy.

Under the tight gaze of her children, Clara walked to the cupboard where she kept the family's emergency fund.

"Here's thirty-six dollars and eighty cents," Clara said. "We'll have to eat chicken for Christmas dinner again this year. I had wanted a ham for us, but no matter."

"You mean we can do it?" Princess asked.

"Well, if you both don't mind going without for Christmas," Clara replied.

"I don't mind at all!" Princess exclaimed, and the two Hogan children ran out the door to the hardware store.

Christmas morning found the Hogan family gathered to open their few gifts. There were three identical boxes under the tree. Ben's heart sank as he realized no one had bought a present for his mother.

"Well, who wants to go first?" Clara asked.

Bursting with anticipation, Princess exclaimed, "Let

Ben go first."

Ben reached for one of the three packages under the tree as everyone watched.

"Ben," Clara said quietly, "I believe you might want to walk over to the cupboard and get the present waiting for you there."

Ben moved toward the cupboard, a little confused but relieved to know his mother had a present under the tree after all.

Inside the cupboard was the hardware store display he had memorized with his wanting: a smooth leather bag with seven brand-new club heads shining over the top. He was afraid to reach for it lest it disappear altogether, and when he touched it for the first time tears formed in his eyes. Hiding his emotions, as usual, he put the bag on his well-worn caddy shoulder and walked in to face his family, each member breathlessly waiting for his response.

A smile crossed Ben's lips when he saw them, and Princess jumped up and down on the old sofa. "He likes it!" she said.

"I told you it was the right thing to do," Royal added.

"Momma," Ben said, "Someday I'm going to be the best golfer in the world for you."

Ben was fifteen years old on the day of the Glen Garden caddy tournament, and it was to be his last one. On his next birthday, if he continued to make money from golf, he would be decreed a professional by the United States Golf Association, a disagreeable label. Professionals were viewed as no better than course bums, while amateurs were considered the gentlemen heroes of the game.

For now, though, Ben was still an amateur, eligible for the appreciation the members of Glen Garden showed their caddies with a nine-hole tournament and dinner. It was to be Ben's first serious challenge against a man who would become his lifelong friend and competitor, Byron Nelson.

Nelson was favored to win the tournament. He was a confident golfer, and he enjoyed showing members and caddies what he could do on a golf course. Everyone at Glen Garden was familiar with Nelson's game and cheered for him to win. In contrast, Ben hid his work on the practice area, silently nursing every stroke. The members knew him only as a hard-working caddy, not as an up-and-coming golfer.

Ben's group of three players teed off with three members serving as their caddies. It was a comical tradition, the well-heeled members serving as bag boys for their own caddies.

To everyone's surprise, Ben played well. His hard work on the practice area had paid off. By the time his group came to the 9th green, he needed a par to finish at two over, 39, which all the spectators thought might be good enough to win.

Ben two-putted for his par, and his fellow players and member-caddies congratulated him on his probable victory. It was not lost on Ben, however, that up until that moment they had not considered him made of championship fiber.

For once, though, Ben had no time to waste on rejection. His spirits were too buoyed at the prospect of winning the tournament prize: a new golf club to add to his growing collection. Right now, this was more important to him than praise.

As the boys finished their rounds, they excitedly spread the word that Ben had finished with a 39. "No one will beat him now," they said.

No one except perhaps Byron Nelson.

Nelson's only hope was to match Ben's score and force a playoff. He faced his last two holes and needed par on each. He easily parred the 8th hole and moved to the 9th tee.

Nelson's drive on the 9th found the right rough. The growing gallery of members and caddies, who had dashed over to watch the finish, groaned with disappointment. They still hoped Nelson, the personal club favorite, would win.

When his second shot came up short of the green, Nelson knew he had to get the ball down in the next two strokes to match Ben's score.

Nelson's third stroke reached the green but left him seventeen feet from the hole for his par. No one in the group of over fifty onlookers expected him to win any longer. It looked like Ben Hogan, the outsider, had won the caddy tournament. Then, while everyone was letting out a long, low, final breath, Nelson sunk the putt.

There had never before been a caddy playoff, and electricity fueled the already excited air as the members poured onto the back nine in a hastily made tournament decision. Ben teed off first and both he and Nelson parred the first two holes. They matched each other hole for hole until the 16th, which Ben bogeyed. The spectators' hopes immediately rested with Nelson, who had never left their hearts as the favorite.

When Nelson bogeyed the 17th hole, it was again a wide-open tournament and the two future champions, one from the haves and one from the have-nots, faced each other on the 18th tee, still even.

Both golfers missed the par-three final green with their tee shots. Tension was collecting its due. Nelson's approach found the green, again leaving him a good-size putt to par the finishing hole. Ben's approach bounced over the bunker fronting the green and rolled to within six feet of the hole.

Once again, Nelson lined up an extraordinary eighteen-foot putt and holed it. But with an easy six-footer it looked as though Ben would turn the match into a second face-off. With the whole gallery holding their breath, he tapped a near-perfect putt toward the cup. Near perfect. In a heartbreaking finish, the ball stopped at the edge of the cup and refused to drop.

For his victory, Nelson was awarded a driving iron while Ben was given a mashie. They looked at each other and grinned, knowing each held the club the other player wanted. A quick swap was arranged, and they smiled as a photographer snapped their picture for history.

But another event, which would not bring a smile to Ben's face, was being arranged behind the scenes. Because the members of Glen Garden Country Club believed that Byron Nelson had a brilliant golfing future, some of them gathered in the deserted pro shop while pictures were being taken to discuss Nelson's status at the club.

"I think we should give him a junior membership," one man said. "That way, he'll be able to use the course when he turns sixteen and quits caddying." He knew that when Nelson's status as a caddy ended, so would his free use of the course.

"What about that other fellow," another voice piped in, "Bennie Hogan. He only lost by one stroke and made a good showing. Shouldn't we do the same for him?"

"Why bother," said a man who expressed everyone's real view, "he won't ever amount to anything. He doesn't have any real talent. Today was just luck, nothing more."

And so, holding his first new driving iron, Ben watched the members he had come to love, who had given him his only opportunity to put food on his mother's table, award an unprecedented junior membership to Byron Nelson, his friend. As he watched the glowing faces surrounding Nelson he realized that, had he won, they would never have given a membership to him.

Once again it was rejection that drove Ben more into himself and more toward the sheer nerve that had almost given him what he now wanted most in life: a tournament victory.

Chapter 3

THE FATES OF BOBBY JONES AND BEN HOGAN ARE LINKED FOREVER

LOCKED OUT OF THE TOP HONORS in the caddy tournament, Ben looked for opportunities no one else wanted. He found an important one in the pro shop where he worked, and it was to lead to his famous mastery of golf mechanics. He found another watching top golfers of the day. One opportunity would turn him into a victim; the other would save his soul.

In the 1920's, almost all golfing equipment was made-to-order in pro shops around the country. Irons, putters, and driver heads were bought from one source, hickory shafts from another. Leather for grips was sometimes acquired at the local tack shop or directly from a tannery.

Shafts were the biggest challenge facing early club makers. Hickory was bought in sticks measuring one inch square by forty to forty-eight inches long. The hickory was then planed and sandpapered into a perfectly round shaft, which was tapered into a hosel and secured with a rivet. Pitch was added to harden it and linseed oil to bring out the grain and season the wood, and then it was ready to pass its final tests. The club had to perform properly or all this effort would be wasted.

Working in the pro shop, Ben participated in the club-making process, performing repairs for the club's members and assisting in making original clubs. Thus, he was able to learn how small changes in equipment produce great differences in performance. It was a simple lesson, but it would affect him for the rest of his life and lead to his tremendous technical skill.

However, in the summer of 1927, when Ben was still fifteen years old, he received another invaluable lesson, this one from a master of golf, Walter Hagen. It was not the kind of lesson a rookie would sign up for; instead, it was a painful lesson in humility.

That year, the PGA Championship was held in Dallas, and Ben was there to watch the best golfers in the world play. He watched as Tommy Armour, Jimmy Thompson, Jock Hutchinson, Leo Diegel, Gene Sarazen and, of course, Walter Hagen, the three-time defending champion, teed off.

Hagen was a wild, brazen thing, a showman who hit crazy shots all over the course and relied on his short game to save his par or birdie and throw his opponent off balance. It was exciting to watch, but it was completely contrary to the way Ben played.

Ben concentrated on hitting fairways and greens in

regulation and sinking his first or second putt. He ignored his playing partners completely, believing golf to be a battle of independence against the course alone. He quickly saw the difference in the two games: The glory was obviously in Hagen's game.

As part of his strategy on the final day of the tournament, Hagen trailed one down in the finals through the 28th hole.

On the 29th, Ben noticed a subtle change in Hagen as he and his opponent, Joe Turnesa, teed off. There were no ropes to control the fans, and Ben was able to hear everything Hagen said and examine everything he did.

Instead of hitting a wild shot, Hagen confidently strolled down the fairway and fired his approach directly at the flag. Ben was amazed to see the crack in Hagen's façade as he dropped his pretentious airs and became a serious player.

On this short par-four 29th hole, Hagen's birdie evened the match.

Walking to the 30th tee, Ben heard Hagen say to his caddy, "Now let's show him how this game is really played."

With a cocky stride, Hagen scored a par on the 30th hole, and Turnesa struggled to match him.

"Gettin' exciting to ya?" Hagen said to no one in particular as he stopped to take a drink of water. "Ah, water!" he exclaimed, wetting his mouth and then spitting it out onto the ground with a wave of his arms.

The show was on again.

Switching back and forth between his role as clown and his role as serious golfer, Hagen scored a masterful birdie on the par-four 31st hole, grabbing the lead for the first time that day.

After two more halved holes, Hagen stood to the side and watched his opponent attempt to match his third shot to the par-five 34th hole. "Gotta give him credit, he's givin' me quite a match," Hagen addressed his audience again. "More than most of 'em do."

Hagen and Turnesa finished stroke for stroke as Hagen fulfilled his promise to win his fourth consecutive PGA Championship.

Ben was so caught up in Hagen's show, he forgot his shyness and asked his new idol for an autograph.

"Sure kid," Hagen agreed, signing a scorecard for Ben. "Do you play golf?"

"Yessir, but not as good as you."

"Let me give you a tip," Hagen began. Ben was all ears as Hagen said, "Never let 'em see you sweat."

The next morning, Ben was stalking his own fifth PGA Championship, swaggering around the practice area with a Hagen jaunt to his step. "Just one more birdie," he bragged out loud, "and victory will be mine!"

"Who do you think you are?" Ben heard a voice say. "The great Walter Hagen?" And it was followed by the laughter of many others. Feeling his face turn red with both embarrassment and anger, Ben suddenly realized the other caddies had been watching him for some time.

"Well . . ." Ben stammered.

"You're not even good enough to clean his clubs," they jeered.

Ben Hogan had been found out, and there was no way around the truth. If he wanted to become a real golfer, he had to stop worrying about gimmicks and face his own technical problems.

He threw himself into each amateur tournament he entered and, at first, it looked as though determination alone would save him. After two rounds under par, with one more to go, Ben found himself in the lead at the West Texas Amateur tournament. All he had to do now was match par on the last eighteen holes, and he would either win or finish in the top three, where all the glory was in amateur events.

Ben couldn't rest the night before the final round. He knew what the tournament meant to his career. A victory would hasten his path ahead of the other golfers from Texas who were proving their worth and moving on to the pro tour.

It was not to be. Ben shot a four over par and finished a disappointing eighth.

Ben shared his disappointment with only one person, a shy, pretty girl he had known since he was twelve years old, Valerie Fox. Although they had never discussed their relationship, it was taken for granted that they would be together one day. Valerie and Ben were inseparable. She followed him from school to the practice tee and her attention suited Ben.

Valerie's father ran the movie theater in Cleburne, a small town near Fort Worth, and in the summer of 1930, when Ben and Valerie were both eighteen years old, a series of newsreels arrived that would paint a fork in the road for Ben. It would be up to the town's quietest girl, unassuming Valerie Fox, to make sure Ben took the right road.

On a day that stood out to Ben Hogan for the rest of

his life, Valerie announced the arrival of the first of these reels.

"Ben," she said, jumping up and down, "Dad says he's got the newsreels that cover Bobby Jones's victories in the British tournaments."

"Do you know if they just cover the ticker-tape parade in New York, or are they about golf, too?" Ben asked, hopeful that the film would show technical strokes.

"I don't think Dad knows what's on the films yet, Ben."

"No, of course not. But do you think he'll let me watch them at night?" Since Ben had given up both his caddy job and his work at the pro shop to remain an amateur, he was forced to work at odd jobs most days and evenings to help feed his family.

"How about at eleven o'clock? I'll have to talk Dad into staying late, but I'm sure he'll be glad to help." Although others, including perhaps Ben himself, were less sure, Valerie saw a champion emerging in his raw determination. It was her first chance to help Ben, to become his partner, and she leapt at it.

At precisely eleven o'clock that night, Valerie's father started the Movietone newsreel. It acted like a rocket booster in Ben's life and set him on course.

The film began with the latest reports about the depression and how people were struggling to make a living. Then, the sports title appeared: Behind it was the moving face of Robert Tyre Jones, Jr.

The story told of Jones winning the British Amateur at St. Andrews and the British Open at Hoylake. It was the first time since John Ball, forty-two years before in 1888, that a golfer had held both titles at the same time.

Jones was shown being helped off the course at St. Andrews by policemen who were charged with keeping him from being mobbed by his thousands of adoring British fans.

Ben and Valerie were moved by what they saw and sat transfixed.

"Did you see the look on his face as the police escorted him off the course, Ben?" Valerie whispered with genuine concern.

"He looked like he had really been through it, didn't he?" Ben replied.

"Do you think he was in any danger?"

"Not real danger. The police were just making sure he didn't get mobbed by all his fans." Ben laughed.

"But did you see that weary look on his face? He looked like he couldn't take another step."

"The rumors are that he loses between ten and fifteen pounds whenever he plays a major tournament."

Now worried for her own man, Valerie challenged Ben. "That's a lot of weight to lose in such a short period of time. I didn't think golf could do that to a person. Does that happen to other players as well?"

"Noooo," Ben drawled as he considered the question. "Nobody else I've ever heard of loses weight like that."

"Well, then why would it happen to Bobby Jones?"

"I don't know." Ben chuckled. "Next time I see him, I'll ask."

"When you start winning your championships, Ben Hogan, I'll make sure you keep your weight. You can't afford to lose a single ounce."

Ben cast Valerie a smile that melted her heart. He

concluded wistfully, "I'm sure you'll take good care of me, Val."

In future years, Ben Hogan would tell the world, "I owe God and my wife Valerie for everything I've gotten." His gratitude started that day, with the first Movietone newsreel, when Valerie persuaded him to go on tour as a professional.

"Ben," she said, "I think you should make a commitment to golf."

"Don't you think I've already made a commitment to golf? It's my whole life."

"No, it's not. Not when you stay away from the pro shop because you're afraid of being called a professional."

"But, Val, what would your Dad think of my being called a golf professional?" Ben pleaded.

"Oh, so that's it. You're afraid of what my father will think." Valerie knew golf professionals were looked down upon by the public as though they were no better than carnival barkers. Amateurs, on the other hand, led by the great Bobby Jones, were revered because they didn't make money from golf. "Did you stop to think about how you're going to support us with golf in the long run if you don't learn how to make money now?"

"I haven't solved that yet, Val," Ben said sharply.

"Well, let's solve that right now. Ben, you have to turn pro. Then you can play in tournaments that will pay you for playing golf. The way you're doing it now, you're in a box, just treading water to keep the glory of an amateur standing that you can't afford. Problem solved, Mr. Hogan," Valerie said, proudly crossing her arms across her chest.

Ben was steamed. He was stubborn, but even to himself, he had to admit Valerie had a point. He crossed his arms, mirroring her stance, and intertwined his fingers in front of him. It was a sign that the Hogan brain was in gear.

"But if I turn professional," he said, "I'll have to pay to enter tournaments, and I almost never have enough money to give to my mother now."

There was more to Ben's dilemma than pure Hogan stubbornness. At the root of his brusqueness was always his large Hogan heart.

Ben quickly spoke again. "But if I win, I'll earn enough to give some to Momma and pay my entry fees in the next tournament." He turned, and smiled at Valerie. "And I'm due to win, aren't I?" Laughing, Ben turned back to the empty movie screen and memories of the inspiring face of Bobby Jones.

The next day, Ben declared himself a pro; he was eighteen years old. It was as simple as deciding to play for money. But with his commitment came hard work, for Ben's lack of natural talent quickly became his roadblock.

"I don't think I'm ever going to solve this game, Val," Ben said one night about a week later. "There are so many variables. For every club, you need a different swing. Just when you finally get one thing right, something else goes out of whack."

"But you're only eighteen, Ben, and you practice more than anyone else. Give the practice a chance to kick in."

"But you wouldn't believe the little things that can go wrong, Val. It may look simple from the outside, but this game must have been invented by someone who thought humans needed to be challenged by something they could never master." Ben paced, running his hand through his hair.

"You have times when you thoroughly master it, Ben. What happens at those times?"

"Well, when the ball is doing what I want it to, it can be pretty terrific." Ben was unused to sharing his feelings with anyone, but Valerie was so supportive that his innermost thoughts began to pour out.

"I get a feeling like nothing else in the world. It's a joy you and I don't feel normally. Someday, Val," he concluded, "I'm going to play the perfect game. I just know it."

Ben's drive was propelling him toward the only credit sportswriters would later give him: perfecting the mechanical side of golf. But there was another not-so-obvious side of Ben developing. His love of the game and his love for Valerie were growing into forces that would one day overshadow all his other victories.

Ben and Valerie eagerly awaited new editions of Movietone newsreels to track the spectacular career of Bobby Jones. In 1930, the four majors were the United States Amateur, the United States Open, the British Amateur, and the British Open. Jones had already won three of them and was headed for the fourth, the U.S. Amateur, to be played at the old Merion Cricket Club in Ardmore, Pennsylvania.

As the world waited for the results of the U.S. Amateur, a subplot to the Merion story was taking shape in which Ben and Valerie were to play starring roles.

The pressure on Jones to win the U.S. Amateur was enormous. Knowledgeable sportswriters, players, and fans believed his win was a sure thing. They treated Jones as a golfing god, not remembering that just a few months before, the grand slam had seemed an impossible feat, something no one even talked about. They ignored what it took to make Jones win: his loss of weight, the sweat pouring off his face, his jittery stutter when he talked. "Win," his fans urged him. "Win at all costs."

Jones fueled their expectations by claiming medalist honors in the Amateur's qualifying rounds, which were used to decide pairings. Shooting rounds of 69 and then 73, he clearly wore the label, "I'm the man to beat."

In private, Bobby Jones was fully aware that any one of the five golfers he would meet in the next four days of match play was capable of catching a hot round and beating him.

The night before the matches were to begin, Jones characteristically could not sleep. He asked his friend, Atlanta sportswriter O.B. Keeler, to walk the course with him. Keeler was one of the leading sportswriters in 1930 but never violated his friendship with Jones by disclosing Jones's secrets. He believed Jones's private life was his own.

Even though it was a black night, full of silent foreboding, they walked the full course, enjoying a little corn whiskey along the way. It was a custom they had shared before the start of each tournament during Jones's grand slam play and one Jones did not want to miss, tonight of all nights.

"We're really creatures of habit, aren't we, O.B.," Jones said. "Even though I played this course in both the '16 and '24 championships, I still feel obligated to keep up with our tradition and walk the course."

"Well, I'd think you'd want to keep a winning formula," O.B. kidded, trying to relax his friend.

As they walked, they passed the corn whiskey back and

forth between them, and O.B. measured his young friend's intake in a fatherly way. A little whiskey calmed Jones's nerves; too much would take away his greatness.

"I'm glad this tournament is at the course where I first played in a national championship," Jones said quietly. "Returning to Merion makes me feel as if my life has come full circle. But . . . " Jones paused for a bit, thinking carefully about what he wanted to say. "But I think the time has come for me to start something else."

Keeler had learned to let his friend talk.

"The pressure of trying to please so many fans is about to end, O.B. For that, I'm glad you won't have to go through this with me anymore. I know it's been tough on you, too, although you've never complained." Like Hogan, Jones was always thinking of someone else's welfare, rarely about his own pain.

Keeler took another small swig from the flask and put it back into his pocket, measuring his response carefully.

"There's no way I would trade this for any other experience in the world, Bob. Being with you has allowed me to live your victories as though they were happening to me, too."

"It sounds as though you're going to miss it." Bobby Jones smiled unseen in the moonless night.

"Just the excitement, Bob. But it's time I got back into writing about other guys." Keeler and Jones both knew there were no other champions in Jones's winner's circle, so high had the top of his mountain grown.

"Yes, it's just as well. My mind and body are glad this is almost over." Jones paused a minute before beginning anew. "Even now, I sometimes can't believe what we've done, O.B. I'm afraid one day I'll wake up, and it'll be gone." Bobby Jones walked through the gathering shadows to see what little was visible of the course.

"It's not about to end for you." O.B. gave his younger friend a wry smile Jones could hear but not see.

"You mean our secret. Don't ever forget O.B., it's not just the whiskey we've shared."

As they passed their final tree on the course, birds scattered into the night air, disturbed by the sound.

The next morning, Jones won the first of his two eighteen-hole matches. His opponent was Ross Somerville, and Jones won easily by a score of five and four.

Of all the matches, Jones feared the eighteen-hole game the most. He knew a lesser golfer was capable of getting hot over such a short distance and shooting a score that would not hold up in a longer match. In fact, that is exactly what had happened in the previous year's Amateur. Jones lost in the first round to Johnny Goodman, an almost unknown golfer out of Nebraska, with a score of three and one. It had been a source of acute disappointment to Jones and had colored every tournament he played in that year.

Now, one year later, Jones faced – and won – his second eighteen-hole match of the day. He defeated Johnny Hoblitzel of Canada, again with a score of five and four. Jones now rested easier, knowing that the most dangerous matches of the tournament were over.

The next two rounds were thirty-six-hole matches, more suited to Jones's skill. For the semifinal round, Jones was to play his toughest opponent yet, Jess Sweetser, a previous winner of the U.S. Amateur and member of many Walker Cup Teams. Sweetser played almost at Jones's level and was always a tough competitor.

But the next day, Jones again ran away with the match, beating Sweetser nine and eight. Afterwards, Jones collapsed in his room and slept until his tee time the following day. This would be his final round of the tournament. He was worn out from the rigors of the past six months and was within one match of writing the final page in the record book that would challenge all future golfers.

O.B. Keeler guarded his friend by sleeping in the hallway on a bench outside Jones's room to make sure he rested undisturbed. O.B. was used to watching an exhausted, spent Jones emerge from his room on the day of the last round of a tournament. However, this time it was different. The grin on Jones's face the next morning told Keeler he had slain a private dragon, and both men marched to the course for the final round.

Ben and Valerie anxiously awaited the results of the match, their ears tuned to the radio for news. They weren't disappointed: Jones handily beat Eugene Homans, another Walker Cup player, eight and seven, and the world let up a roar in tribute.

What the radio didn't tell Ben and Valerie was that their idol shared Ben's acute shyness and lack of confidence. These two traits were not all they would share. Their secret would also bind them inextricably to one another, like two strands of the same string.

Two months later, Bobby Jones again shocked the world.

Looking for Ben late one night, Valerie found him in her father's theater, in the front row, viewing Jones's old Movietone newsreels.

"How many times has Steve run this film for you?" Valerie asked, snuggling into the seat next to Ben.

"I really don't know," Ben laughed. "I've lost count."

"Look at how he's extending his thumbs down the shaft, Val," Ben said without taking his eyes off the big screen. "He makes changes he doesn't even notice himself."

"Do his little changes mean anything to the swing, Ben?" Valerie knew of Ben's growing obsession with his swing.

"It all means something, Val. I just haven't figured out what."

"There's something I need to tell you," Ben whispered, a glazed look on his face. "Something I sense about these films."

"I'm all ears, Mr. Hogan."

"Well, when I watch the films, I get the eerie feeling that Bobby Jones is talking directly to me. I know it must sound crazy, but that's one of the reasons I watch them. I feel as though he's talking directly to me. It's spooky, Val, but I feel like I know him, like I've already met him."

And then the dream was over. Only two months after completing his grand slam win, Bobby Jones abruptly retired from competitive golf at the age of twenty-eight. He retired for two reasons that he would tell no one: because of the ultimate secret of golf and to make room for Ben Hogan.

Chapter 4

THE MAGIC OF A REPETITIVE SWING

A PART OF BOBBY WAS BORN in Ben Hogan at the same time it was retired in Jones. It was almost as if the skill was transmitted from Jones to Hogan through the mystical threads that connect all objects in the universe.

In 1932, after he deliberately faded his own star, Jones made a series of eighteen instructional films capturing his enthusiasm for golfing fundamentals. On the screen, Bobby Jones taught popular film stars who were so thrilled to get a personal lesson from him that they appeared without a fee. He showed the game's fundamentals to the likes of W.C. Fields, Douglas Fairbanks, and the Marx brothers.

When Valerie's father learned of the films, he mentioned them to her. "Warner Brothers has just made a number of instructional films with Bobby Jones. Should I order them for Ben?"

"Right away, Dad. Ben'll be so excited." Valerie paused, and in a voice so soft it sounded as if she was talking to herself, she said, "You know, one day, I think Bobby Jones will have something to do with Ben's career."

Back in their favorite seats at the movie house, Ben and Valerie watched each film as it arrived. Ben analyzed the films for details he could use. He was obsessed with finding every nuance of the perfect golf swing, as if he could become a purely mechanical genius and ignore the rest of the game.

"Look," Ben pointed out to Valerie. "Jones is doing little things he doesn't mention in the film."

"Does it mean something?" Valerie questioned.

"It all means something. Every little change has an impact on how you use the club and on the results you get." Ben held his breath, silently analyzing what he had just seen on the screen. He let it out with a sigh, "I just wish I knew what it all meant."

Jones made golf look easy, but it was not easy for Ben. His practice became entwined with the movie screen as he tried Jones's techniques on the driving range and then watched the film again to make sure he got it right. While he waited for the next film to arrive, Ben repeated what he had learned, over and over, trying to ingrain the responses into his muscles. He hoped he could train his muscles to perform automatically by sheer force of repetition.

Ben was developing the repetitive swing.

Late one night, Valerie found Ben in the theater, in the front row, viewing Jones's film on how to recover from bad lies.

Ben was transfixed by the rolling image of Bobby Jones.

"Stop the film, stop the film!" Ben cried out.

The projectionist obeyed.

"Look at that," Ben exclaimed. "Look at how Jones

is pulling his left thumb back up to the shaft. He seems to be doing it automatically." Ben lowered his voice and wrinkled his brow. "But he doesn't mention the change he's making during the talking portion."

"Will such a little change really make a difference?" Valerie asked.

"I haven't tried it yet, but I think it will."

The next morning found Ben on the practice range. Wanting to view his new discovery, Valerie joined him an hour later.

"Watch this," Ben said as he hit shot after shot directly at his target. "Remember that shortened thumb. That's what helps to keep the club under control during the back-swing."

"You mean that little change is allowing you to hit those balls so well?"

"Yep. I've been trying to find the perfect swing, so that I can repeat it time after time. Bobby Jones just showed me how to do it."

Another film in the series arrived the next day. Ben and Valerie patiently watched as Jones demonstrated shots in a strange outfit that was half black and half white. The purpose of the two colors was to show the effect of the two sides of the body during the swing, which was being shown in slow motion.

"Whoa, whoa," Ben yelled out to Steve. "Roll it back just a half minute."

"Did you see it, Val? Did you see it?"

"See what, Ben?"

"The club head. Watch the club head." Ben had Steve roll the film back one more time.

"I don't believe it," Ben said as they watched the rerun portion of the film. "Everything I've known until now about hitting the ball was based on the hands moving through slightly before the club head. But in slow motion, this film shows it's the other way around – the club head hits the ball before his hands get there."

On the practice range, Ben demonstrated the shot for Valerie. He hit drive after drive down the right side of the range and drew it back into the left middle of the target area.

"What am I looking for, Ben?" Valerie asked.

"Look at the way I'm able to extend my swing by keeping the club low to the ground on the takeaway," Ben said, hitting another shot right where he wanted it to land. "I now hit a longer shot. You'd think I was six feet two, instead of five feet nine."

"Oh, I get it. You'll be able to land all your balls on the fairways and greens." Valerie had heard Ben mutter "fairways and greens" many times when he practiced, and she knew this was the ultimate goal behind his obsession in developing the perfect swing.

"Straight and far, Val, straight and far," Ben said as he added another chant to his practice session.

"Now all I have to do is duplicate this swing. I have to train my muscles to know what to do every time I pick up a club."

Ben rearranged his practice sessions to match his muscle training theories. During each practice, he hit every club in his bag twelve times. Three shots were fades, three were draws, three were high shots, and the last three were low windcheaters. Already, Ben knew each club had to perform individually to avoid wasting shots.

With his stellar practice sessions, Ben now felt that he had enough new skills to use in competitive play but found he was handicapped by low-paying Texas tournaments. The real action was in the big pro tournaments around the country, which often paid as much as fifteen hundred dollars for first place. That's where Ben's heart led him. To be the best golfer in the world, he had to prove himself against the best, and the best weren't all located in Texas.

Valerie, too, realized Ben had to leave Texas, and she wanted to help by contributing to Ben's tour savings fund. Ben disagreed.

"It's the man's job to make the living. I'm the one who's responsible for making enough to support us and join the tour."

"But Ben," Valerie argued, "it makes sense for me to contribute. That way we'll achieve our goals more quickly."

"Oh great," Ben responded. "So it's all decided. I get to sit by and watch you work, so that I'll have enough money to try the tour. That doesn't leave much room for me to make decisions about my own future, does it?"

Valerie was surprised. He would have to change, she realized. He needed her help.

"Val," Ben continued, "I know I can do it. I want you to trust me to do it alone."

Valerie paused for what seemed like an eternity as she planned her strategy. When she finally spoke, it was in a very soft voice. "If we work together, Ben, we can solve our problems faster. You know, you're going to have to let someone penetrate that thick shell of yours someday. It might as well be now."

"So you think I should learn to accept help," he said, twisting his face in resignation.

"I don't know why this is so important, Ben. It just is. Maybe we'll find out together someday, but for now, I just know I have to help you."

Ben budged, but only a little. "How about if I put up the money for now, and we'll see how it goes?"

Valerie laughed. "I have never met anyone as stubborn as you! Just like the horses with their blinders on, you can't see anything except what you're after. That's an admirable trait, Ben Hogan, and it'll help you win tournaments. But, you'll also find out you can't become the best without the help of other people. That's what being the best is all about." Valerie didn't know how prophetic her words would turn out to be.

As the days passed, in silent commitment to their goal, Ben and Valerie squeezed out time to talk about their future. Their plan was to send Ben out on tour to win enough for them to get married. Later when enough money had been earned, Valerie would travel with him.

"You know, Val, one big win of fifteen hundred dollars would give us enough to live on for an entire year," Ben commented one day. "If only I could do in a tournament what I can do on the driving range – and make the results of my practice permanent."

"Your practice sessions are already wonderful, Ben. Why are you always so hard on yourself?"

"Here's the problem. Sometimes I spend three hours hitting perfect drives and then, wham, I'm on the course and I can't even keep one on the fairway. This game would be so much easier if I only had to learn something one time. Why should I have to learn and then relearn something I've already worked on?"

"Because you're human, playing a human game?" Valerie offered.

"But why is it so hard? Having hit a perfect shot once, it makes sense that it would be easier the second time. But that's not what happens." Ben squirmed under the pressure of trying to master precision golf, and as he walked he rubbed the back of his head as though trying to jog his memory of the perfect shot.

"The imperfection is what makes golf the challenge that you love," Valerie explained. "That's the intrigue. If you ever do master it, do you think that you'd still really enjoy it?"

"Of course I would!" he countered. "Then, I'd spend one entire year going around to all the tournaments, winning and setting new records." Ben puffed up his chest at the vision. "Perfection would be my middle name," he said with a broad smile.

Valerie had an idea. "Why not measure your progress on a regular basis, Ben?"

"I'm already doing that with my practice sessions. The problem is that I discover something one day, and forget it the next."

"I've got what you need, Ben Hogan. I'm surprised you didn't think of it yourself. It's so simple." Valerie rummaged in her purse and fished out a little black notebook.

"A notebook?" Ben asked in wonder.

"Yes, to help you keep track of things. It's broken down by

date, and it even has an address area you can use to keep track of tournaments. And, it's good for the whole year." Valerie was very proud of herself. Her contribution would later prove to be even more valuable than the money she earned.

"I think you've got something here," Ben turned the notebook over and over in his hands. "I can use those little scoring pencils to write down what I do when I hit a perfect shot, and then later when I'm playing, I can use the notebook to refresh my memory!" His excitement grew. "The notebook and pencil will fit just fine in my back pocket, too, so I'll never be without it." Ben was already on his way out to the practice range with his newest secret when he remembered to thank Valerie.

"How can I ever thank you, Val?"

"By becoming everything you were meant to be, Ben, and letting me share it with you."

On the practice range, Ben experimented and then recorded what he learned in his little black book. It was the first of many black books that would eventually contain his private secrets about golf. All except the final secret.

By 1932, when he was twenty years old, Ben was ready for the tour. He and Valerie had saved enough money to buy a secondhand Hudson Roadster and thus launch Ben's competition on the pro tour. He was shooting under par on all the courses around Fort Worth, and he believed he would do the same once he got on tour.

He was wrong. If love had helped Ben's game, then loneliness destroyed it.

In those days, there was no such thing as an official tour. Players simply showed up at an advertised event, paid the entry fee, and received a tee-off time. The wives of a few experienced tour pros had managed to get some tournaments scheduled consecutively on neighboring courses to help cut down on travel time and expenses. Thus, the events of the early thirties began to draw a better field and often included the top traveling golfing stars of the day.

Small tournaments usually had a total payout of $3500, while larger events might pay as much as $7500 with payouts going all the way down to the twentieth spot.

Ben's contemporaries were passing him by, and he knew it. He had grown up with Byron Nelson, who was already winning money on the pro tour. Ralph Guldahl from Dallas had moved to Hollywood, California, and was the fastest success story out of Texas. He began winning the year before, in 1931, as an amateur in the Santa Monica Open. Lloyd Mangrum was already living in Los Angeles, and Jimmy Demaret had a tour victory in San Francisco. Everyone was moving up except Ben.

On top of this, Nelson and Guldahl were qualifying for the U.S. Open each year. Guldahl would in fact become runner-up for the title the next year in 1933 at the age of twenty-two.

In the spring on 1932, Los Angeles was host to a group of tournaments arranged by the wives of the pro tour golfers. Over the span of four weeks, seven tournaments would be held within a few hours' drive from Los Angeles. These included an Invitational at Wilshire, a Pro-Am at Hillcrest, the Los Angeles Open, and the Long Beach Open, as well as three other smaller affairs.

A few events were two-day tournaments while others lasted three or four days. Some tournaments played seventy-two holes, others fifty-four holes, and the odd one played thirty-six. A tournament could be held Thursday through Saturday with a thirty-six-hole finish on the last day, while the next event might run Monday through Thursday with eighteen holes played each day.

There was no such thing as a thirty-six-hole cut. Once you paid your money, you had the right to play the entire tournament, regardless of your score.

Ben and Valerie decided that Los Angeles would be Ben's first venture onto the pro golf tour.

"I'm going to miss you," Valerie sighed. "I won't even know how to get in touch with you."

Although Valerie did not want Ben to see how sad she was, a small tear escaped and rolled down her cheek. She quickly brushed it away, for she knew the tear meant more than sadness at their separation. In case he failed, she wanted to be there to comfort him.

Ben didn't see Valerie's sadness; he was still starry-eyed with dreams of glory. He suggested a wild extravagance: the telephone where Valerie worked.

"Let's use the phone at Riggsbee's Drug Store," he said. "Mr. Riggsbee can let you know I've called, and then I'll call back fifteen minutes later."

"That's so expensive, Ben. I don't want you to use up all your money talking to me. You'll need it to support yourself on the road." Always realistic, Valerie knew Ben's wins and the money he earned from them might have to stretch as far as they would soon be.

"Well, how about once a week after I finish a tournament to tell you how well I did?" Ben expected to win and win big. He honestly didn't believe money would be a problem for him once he got out on tour.

"That would be great," she sighed. "Gosh, Los Angeles is such a long way away."

"First California, then New Mexico, Nevada, Arizona, and finally back to Texas. How about if I come home with a trophy – or two?" Ben laughed as he hooked his arm around the only girl he would ever love.

Ben's excitement fueled his trip, pushing him to beat his scheduled arrival time. Strangely, however, every mile seemed to take him away from his dream, not closer to it.

To stay awake on the road, Ben focused on the tar between the concrete sections on the highway. They expanded during the heat of the day and made a pinging noise as he rode over them. At first, he counted the pings, but after counting into the hundreds, Ben chided himself at the ridiculous exercise. He tried to stop counting, but the pings had acquired a life of their own. Soon, they were pinging with the disappointment he had yet to experience.

"You haven't won yet at home, and now, you expect to win in California, and at a higher level?" he muttered to himself. Loneliness had begun its relentless chip into Ben's confidence.

Ben finally arrived in Los Angeles and was amazed to find a much bigger city than he had imagined. Like a lot of Texans who possessed a bigger-than-life slice of pride, Ben believed that being born and raised in Texas would prepare him for everything else in the world. It didn't.

The sight of Los Angeles hit Ben with the force of a hot wind, leaving him tired and dry. There were fruit stands, people, cars, homes, and stores on every corner and in every direction. Ben drove into a gas station and asked for directions to his first golf course.

"Hi there," Ben said in his friendly Texas drawl. "I'm looking for the Riviera Country Club. Can you help me out?"

"What do I look like, the answer man?" The attendant hadn't even looked up from the engine he was hunched over. Ben wasn't worth a look.

This is definitely not Texas, Ben thought as he returned to his car. He found his way alone.

After registering at Riviera, Ben discovered the course wouldn't be available for practice play until the afternoon prior to the tournament. Some of the members had complained about the condition of the course after the previous year's tournament and wanted to minimize wear and tear. His early arrival now meant nothing, Ben realized. Sadly, he settled into the cheapest motel he could find to wait.

Two days later, Ben arrived at the course for his practice round and was told that the members had again changed their policy. They had decided to disallow practice to all players, giving an advantage to golfers who had played the course in the past.

Ben was, of course, not one of them.

Ben's next blow came when he was introduced to his caddy for the tournament, John.

"How well do you know the course?" Ben asked hopefully.

The caddy shuffled his feet and stammered, "I've only caddied here once. But I'm sure I can get you through." Seeing the crestfallen look on Ben's face, he added, "I really need the work Mr. Hogan. I've got a wife and two kids to support, and without caddying, I'd be without work. I really need the five dollars."

"Five dollars! A day? You mean that's what caddies out here make?"

"Yessir."

Maybe I should have stayed a caddy, Ben thought.

Not being able to play the course added to Ben's anxiety. Rather than rely on John's meager knowledge, Ben decided to walk the course. Taking in every sight, he could tell the course would play long during the coming tournament because of the well-watered lush grass. The greens were cut the way he preferred, close and quick, but nothing else matched his playing experience in Texas. The majority of the doglegs were contrary to Ben's natural ball flight pattern, and the course was lined with trees. He knew he had his work cut out for him.

As his eyes took in the long sight down the fairway, throngs of people were all he saw. With so many people, he thought, there won't be any space left to play golf.

For the first time in his life, Ben's hands shook as he teed up his ball. Although his nervous shot was partly heeled, Ben's drive was acceptable to him. He was grateful it had stayed on the fairway.

His hands calmed on the second hole, but his internal system continued to roar with disapproval. John, his caddy, saw that Ben was desperately trying to recover his game, but he was powerless to help him.

As shot after shot went astray, Ben felt as if he were playing a script he was unable to stop. His nerves were torn, knocking his body out of kilter. Nothing he did worked anymore, and Ben finally accepted his fate. His first tournament round was one of the worst eighteen-hole scores he had ever posted.

Ben picked up his bag and, rather than leave it at the course, he took it with him. In a daze, he drove to his rented roadside cabin and collapsed on his bed. He curled up under the blankets in his lonely little room. He was alone in the world, and he knew it.

The trip to the golf course the next morning was drudgery to Ben. He was terrified of teeing off in front of the crowd, and he knew he would not be in charge of his body again. In front of all those strangers, he felt like a stranger to himself. There was nowhere to hide.

Ben's caddy greeted him with a big smile. He had expected Ben to quit, so he was glad to have another chance to make five dollars.

The course wasn't as full this second day. The movie stars had all gone back to their glamorous lives, leaving Ben alone with his golfing struggles. Realizing that things were a bit more to his liking, Ben settled down.

Going through his practice routine, Ben saw that his actions were normal, although his rhythm wasn't quite right. With effort, he found he could produce a swing that was close to what it should be.

Just as things looked like they might return to normal, however, a new horror joined Ben on the practice tee: Joe Kirkwood, a trick-shot artist from Australia, who started giving demonstrations on how to hit unusual shots. Following Joe was an emcee with a megaphone, who blaringly announced every movement to the crowd.

Ben beat a hasty retreat to the putting green, but his hands started to tremble again.

His drive off the first tee was shaky, but slightly less shaky than the day before. At least he was playing golf. As Ben looked down the fairway, seeing only a few spectators, he glimpsed a vision of his familiar sanctuary: the green, newly cut grass that had always been his emotional refuge.

Ben's second round went better, but the real Hogan was a long way from making his appearance. At the end of play, he had bettered his previous day's score by seven strokes. "I'm still playing lousy golf, but at least I'm headed in the right direction," Ben told himself with as much warmth as he could muster.

Valerie was not expecting a call from Ben until after the tournament, but he needed to talk to her. He put in a call to Riggsbee's Drug Store and asked Mr. Riggsbee to alert Valerie. Fifteen minutes later, she was on the line.

"Valerie?" Ben's voice shook.

"What's wrong? I wasn't supposed to get a call from you for two more days."

Ben's face was hot with shame, and he was glad Valerie couldn't see him. He had let her down, and he knew it.

"Physically, I'm okay. Mentally, it's another story. That's why I'm calling."

"Did you play in the tournament at all?" Valerie asked, sensing the worst by the sad tone in his voice.

"If you could call what I did playing. To be blunt, I've

been doing very poorly and I'm not sure what to do."

"What's wrong, Ben? I've never heard you so low. Surely anything that's wrong can be fixed."

"If I had known what the pro tour was really like, I wouldn't have come. This is completely different than anything I've ever seen. It's thrown my game off. I haven't hit a decent shot since I've been here. Hell, Val, I don't even know when I will hit a decent shot."

Valerie tried to buoy his spirits. "Oh, Ben, it's just your first tournament. Try to enjoy the course and do your best. That's all you can expect from a new experience."

"But Val, you wouldn't believe what this place is like. There are movie stars and big-name golfers walking all over the place. There are thousands of people watching everything you do. And, the reporters. They ask you questions just when you're getting ready to hit your shot, and photographers snap pictures in the middle of your swing. With all the noise, it's even hard to remember what you scored on a hole let alone keep up with your competitor's score."

Valerie shuddered at the frightening mental picture Ben had painted. The noise and distraction were particularly difficult for a shy man like Ben, she realized.

Quickly she chose a tack, hoping it was the right one. "Remember when we talked about how we all have different things to overcome?"

"I don't see how that applies here. This isn't a tournament, it's a carnival. I don't see how anyone does it. Maybe this isn't for me."

"Ben, dear, you remind me of another golfer."

"Who?"

"Bobby Jones. In the newsreels, didn't he look strange

after each tournament? As though he had been jostled around? Do you think you're experiencing the same problems he had?"

"I think you've hit on something." Ben brightened immediately at Valerie's logic. "This is exactly what Jones must have gone through. Now I know why he lost all that weight. His nerves gave up on him, just like mine are doing."

Ben's spirits steamrolled into optimism.

"If Bobby Jones could still play golf under these conditions, I guess I can, too."

Valerie caught her sob before Ben could hear it, just in time to hear him say, "I miss you, Val, and I wish you were here."

Ben got a restful night's sleep after talking with Valerie and finished his first tournament. He played better the last two days. Not much better, but better.

After the tournament was over, Ben walked the course to understand what had taken place. The golf course was now almost at peace without the people, and Ben saw what the course designer had been trying to do with each hole. It was meant to be poetry; this combination of drives and iron shots and putts. Ben told himself that, someday, he would be back and he would enjoy this course, win or lose.

Ben's next tournament was a two-day Pro-Am event at Ingleside Golf Club. Ben arrived at the course two days early, hoping to be able to play the course. His hopes were met with success.

By the time the tournament started, Ben felt ready. First-tee jitters struck him again, however, when he saw the crowd of people lining the fairway.

After posting his first-round score, Ben thought that his

second tournament was turning out just like the first. He considered calling Valerie but decided, "I'm here alone. I'll just have to get used to it."

Ben wondered how he compared to the touring professionals he had seen. In only two events, he had already met Tommy Armour, Gene Sarazen, Walter Hagen, Olin Dutra, Bill Mehlhorn, Leo Diegel, Craig Wood, and Paul Runyan. He really felt good when he met Runyan, who was smaller than he was. Although Ben was not a short man, he had a smallish, five-feet, nine-inch frame, and Runyan made him realize you didn't have to be a big man to be on tour.

Ben played on with his newfound handicaps. Whether it was people, first-tee jitters, too-soft beds, or lack of confidence, he struggled. Through tournament after tournament, his name avoided the leader board. He would do well for a hole or two and sometimes finish around par, but overall, tournament golf was a struggle to him.

After five weeks in California, Ben was exhausted, financially and mentally.

He made one last call to Valerie.

"I just want to come home," he admitted. "It's been a nightmare. Right now, I have just enough money to make it back."

"Just get home safely," Valerie consoled. "We'll figure out what to do when you get home."

Before he hung up, Ben's raw nerves announced the real purpose of his call. "I'm sorry I failed."

The silence of Ben's three-day ride back home gave him time to reflect on his poor performance. He fastidiously went back over the details of each tournament. More and more, he came to the conclusion that he hadn't played well because he hadn't been able to get into his game. No matter how many excuses he made, it all came down to the same thing. Not being able to concentrate had led to his pitifully poor results.

As would become his habit after each tournament, Ben analyzed his scores and realized that his final round scores were always the best. His scoring chart ran a straight path. His first round scores were high, followed by a slightly lower second round, and then somewhat competitive third and fourth rounds.

It was futile, Ben thought, to get better at the end of each tournament, just to falter again at the beginning of the next. And each day's problems were directly related to how uncomfortable he felt. But, he realized with a sigh, feelings were not supposed to be part of the game of golf.

How on earth did Bobby Jones do it? he wondered.

Chapter 5

HOGAN DISCOVERS HIS BIGGEST HANDICAP

"VAL, DO YOU REMEMBER the time I was practicing at the high school and the band showed up? Remember how they damned near blasted me off the field? My hands shook and I couldn't concentrate at all. Well, that's what the tour was like." Ben had arrived home from his grueling trip.

"I'm glad you didn't give up, Ben. This is something we can solve together."

"I don't know. Maybe I'm just not cut out to be a pro. This one seems to be beyond me."

"But not beyond us, Ben. Besides, what will you do? Be a caddy all your life? Nonsense. Everything in golf is solvable. You've taught me that with all your practice sessions."

"But, Val, how do you practice concentration?"

"Well, let's try a concentration exercise."

"A what?"

"A concentration exercise. Since your mind is the

problem, let's work on your mind. I was reading an article in *Reader's Digest* the other day, and it said mental exercises can help you overcome problems."

Valerie's comment piqued Ben's interest, and he asked what the article recommended.

"Sit down on the ground and close your eyes. In your imagination, see yourself walking onto the first tee in front of thousands of spectators just like you did at your tournaments."

Ben did as he was told and said, "I see it, Val, but I don't like it. How can this help me?"

"Stay in the scene. Keep it in your mind even though it makes you uncomfortable."

"Well, I didn't like it then and I don't like it now."

"Yes, I understand that." Valerie laughed. "Just be a little patient. Now, watch yourself teeing off in front of all those people – but this time, don't let them bother you. Hit your best shot."

"Okay I'll give it a try. I'm looking at all the faces and . . . ugh! But I am hitting a good shot."

"Now try it again. Only this time, try to make those people go away. Or pretend they aren't there."

"Alright, I'm at the tee again. They're there, but you know, you're right – I don't feel as nervous. I'm concentrating on my swing instead of them. I think you've discovered a solution, Val!"

"I've got another idea."

"Really? What is it?" Ben was now eager for all the mind control exercises Valerie could invent.

"Remember that high school band?"

"Yeah, they're the ones who started all this."

"That's right, and they can finish it for you, too. Why don't you try practicing within earshot of them? I'll bet you'll soon discover how to tune them out."

"You mean, practice with the distraction instead of trying to avoid it?" Ben considered the possibility. "Gee, Val, I think it might work."

Although he felt strange doing it, Ben made mental practice a part of his regular practice sessions. He sat for long periods of time seeing himself tee off in front of thousands of Californians. Then, he hit balls, striking each club in his bag twelve times. Whenever he could get time off from work at the pro shop, the job he returned to after his miserable tour experience, he practiced in front of the high school band.

"I must look really strange out there," he told himself the first time he sat down on the band field to perform his mental imaging. "There can't be another pro alive who's doing this."

Despite his fears about how he looked to others, Ben continued. At first, he tried desperately to ignore the music in the background.

It was impossible to do. Each time he heard a horn or a drum beat, he froze, and then hurriedly made his shot. Soon, however, he realized he was rushing because of the volume of the noise, and he concentrated on slowing himself down.

Neither Ben nor Valerie knew what effect Ben's mental practice would have on his game. They got their first chance to find out when the golf professional at Glen Garden Country Club told Ben about a little tournament at a private course in Galveston. It only paid through twelve places, but Ben jumped at this chance to get back into competitive golf.

Ben arrived in Galveston and paid his ten-dollar entry fee. To his surprise, the tournament had drawn plenty of fans. The crowds were not as big as the ones in California, but they would do as a test for his new mental practice.

After two rounds of 73 and 71, Ben was tied for seventh place. To celebrate, he spent even more time in the practice area, methodically exercising his mind and then hitting each club over and over. That night, when he laid his head down on the pillow in his roadside cabin, it finally hit him. This was his first really good chance to win.

Early the next morning, he called Riggsbee's Drug Store and left a message for Valerie.

"Tell her I'm in the running."

Valerie was at Riggsbee's when he called at the end of the tournament. She had been there all afternoon, anxiously awaiting his call and the results of their hard work. Finally, the call came in.

"We did it!" Ben exclaimed. "We won."

When he finally arrived home, Ben asked Valerie the question that had been burning in his mind for several months. It wasn't about marriage, though; it was more important.

"Val, I want you to come out on tour with me."

"Is this your way of proposing?" They had always talked about getting married but never formally.

"Of course." Ben's mind was already two steps ahead. "I always assumed we'd get married one day so, yes, I guess I am proposing. The players who bring their wives with them on tour do really well."

"So you only want to get married to play better golf?" Valerie teased.

"No, no, that's not it at all," Ben stammered. "You know what I mean. Golf isn't just my life, it's our life."

Ben looked at the woman he loved and poured out his heart, "For just one year, I want to be the best. The very best golfer in the world. I'll have a chance to do that if you'll come with me. Will you do it, Val?"

"Yes, Ben, yes. I'll marry you for all the reasons you've given me and a few of my own. Am I to assume we'll have our honeymoon on the road at our first tournament?"

"That's a great idea!"

Ben and Valerie were married in a small, simple ceremony filled with love. Their families and friends had already taken their commitment for granted, and now they were free to follow Ben's dream of becoming the best golfer in the world.

By 1936, just one year after getting married, Ben and Valerie had managed to save $1400 and were ready to take off for the tour. Their plan was to join the summer tour on the east coast and follow it to California, then across the south through Arizona, Texas, and Louisiana, and on to Florida, finishing in Augusta and Pinehurst.

This time, Ben and Valerie were not expecting miracles. Their goal was to finish "in the money," placing in the top fifteen in order to earn their way across country. However, like most of the journeymen golfers, Ben failed.

A sheepish Ben reported his scores after each tournament with these words, "Sorry, hon, out of the money again." He didn't try to vary his speech. Why bother?

Through Virginia and Maryland, it was always the same.

In Pennsylvania, a new face arrived from the backwoods of Virginia. Sam Snead joined the struggling tour, bragging about all the wins he would have as soon as he "got things adjusted." Jealously, Ben saw that Snead had the great swing he himself longed to possess, but he also realized with a smug air that Snead would probably wind up on the list of strugglers, for the same top pros won the money each week.

Valerie never showed her disappointment at Ben's failure, however, not even when Snead finished in the money in Hershey, Pennsylvania. She always believed it was just a matter of time before the discoveries Ben made in his practice sessions paid off. One day, she knew, Ben would turn the corner and no one would ever beat him again. No matter how much Valerie boosted, however, Ben's spirits sank along with their bank account.

To make it to the end of the tour, the newlyweds ate oranges. At first, the oranges merely supplemented meals, serving as breakfast instead of eggs and toast at a roadside café. By the time Ben and Valerie arrived in California, however, oranges were all they had left to eat – peeled, squeezed, or sliced, it was oranges. If Ben didn't start winning in California, they would be forced to head back to Texas, perhaps never to return to the tour.

In the latter part of March, Ben finished out of the money again in San Diego. They had just enough money left to get to Oakland for one final, four-day tournament. It was almost time to call it quits.

Ben and Valerie drove through Oakland looking for the best room rate, and they found it just a few miles from the course. It wasn't the best area of Oakland, and the owner of the motel charged guests ten cents to park in his protected parking area. Ben couldn't afford the extra charge, so he parked his Buick down the street in an empty lot.

The night before the Oakland tournament, Valerie fell asleep to the sound of Ben putting golf balls across the floor of their cabin. They had agreed to spend $1400 and, although his guilt at not winning money felt like an extra bag on his shoulders, he pushed on. Well into the night, Ben practiced a new putting stroke he had discovered during that day's practice session, dutifully referring to his notes in the little black book.

After three rounds, Ben was in eighteenth place. The tournament paid through fifteen positions, and he knew he had a good chance of winning a paying spot.

On the morning of the last day of the tournament, Ben walked out of his motel room and down the street to retrieve his car. The sight of what he found in the parking lot shocked him, and he ran back to the hotel room.

"My God, Valerie, some bastard has taken the tires off our car! The rear end is sitting on concrete blocks. They even took the jack!

"I have no way to get to the tournament. We can't even afford to buy tires to get us home. What are we going to do?" It was the supreme moment for the nonplaying partner of the Hogan team, when time stood still and Valerie could see their fork in the road stenciled in the heavy air around her. She knew what they had to do.

"Ben," she said calmly, "this is nothing more than another concentration exercise. What we're going to do is get you to the course and then you're going to place in the money today."

Ben caught a ride to the course with Sam Snead, the rookie who had already bypassed him on the tour. Ben sat in Snead's car, slumped in defeat.

"Well, Ben," Snead said, trying to cheer him on, "at least they didn't take y'alls clubs."

This guy really doesn't understand anything, Ben thought. Everything's so easy for him.

"It shouldn't cost you much to get the tars replaced," Snead offered cheerfully.

"Right now, anything is too much," Ben said curtly.

"Ya know, Ben, what y'all need is a win."

Ben looked at Snead in silent disbelief, knowing that if he spoke at all, he might not be able to hold himself back.

There would be no time for practice on this final morning because Ben was late. He had just two minutes to rush to the first tee before being disqualified. While Ben was teeing up his first shot, Valerie was praying in their motel room.

"Please, God, don't let this be the end of the long trial Ben has put himself through." She tried not to think about money, but in the end she just waited, eating their ever-present oranges.

As Ben teed off, he felt the stalking pressure. Valerie's presence was nearer to him than the crowds in the galleries, though, willing him to succeed. He wanted to win more than ever before, for Valerie, for the other losing golfers who needed hope, for his own hope.

Ben took a deep breath and told himself to concentrate on each shot, for that's what the game meant to him. Finding his love of shotmaking for the first time on tour, Ben addressed his ball. At first he was consistent with his past performances on tour: technically correct but lacking the fire of a winner. But the more he concentrated on each shot, the more his game improved. For once, drama was having a positive effect on Ben.

As his third birdie in a row dropped on the 12th hole, Ben quickly tried to add up his score. Have I still got a chance? He thought. Just as quickly he reminded himself to stay with his game, shot by shot. "If I stay with my game, the final results will speak for themselves," he said, with more courage than he felt.

On the par-five 16th hole, Ben dropped his fourth birdie putt of the day. Just two more to go and I might win something, he thought.

The par-three 17th hole gave him trouble, and he settled for a par. The champion in Ben was at last emerging. His drive on the dogleg left, 18th hole, was true and slightly drawn as Ben moved to the finish line. As he sank his putt, tears welled in his eyes, and the pent-up emotion ran out of his limbs like melted butter. He knew he had given it his best shot, even if he hadn't won anything.

Ben slowly went over his scorecard, added up his 68 again and again, and finally turned it in.

At the motel, Valerie had fallen asleep. She didn't know whether it was from nervous fatigue or from hunger. She awoke when she heard Ben's key in the door.

"Have you got a dollar for the cab?" Ben said as his cab driver waited to be paid.

Valerie handed Ben her last five-dollar bill, and Ben shocked her by telling the cab driver to keep the change.

"Ben!" she shouted, "you just gave him a four dollar tip! We might need that money."

"Not anymore," Ben grinned, "not when you hear how we did today."

"Ben," she breathed, "do you mean you won?"

"No, honey, not that good." Ben recounted the details of the day. "If any one of three putts had dropped, we would have been in sole possession of second. And if all three had dropped, I would be out there right now playing my first playoff in front of hundreds of people."

"Dear," Valerie said, slightly exasperated, "exactly how well did we do?"

"We tied for second with Harry Cooper, thanks to Harry having an off day and, oh my gosh, I forgot to wait for my check."

"How much do you think it will be?" a very relieved Valerie asked.

"Three hundred and eighty-five dollars."

"Three hundred and eighty-five dollars! Oh God, Ben, we're rich. Now we can make it to the next tournament in Phoenix."

"Val, we're never going to be in this spot again. That I can promise you. Never again."

Ben and Valerie borrowed some money from their overnight landlord, who knew Ben would be picking up a fat check in the morning, and they treated themselves to a steak dinner.

Years later, when he was seventy-three years old, after facing more challenges on tour than any other golfer, Ben commented, "That $385 check was the biggest check I ever received. No matter how much money I've ever made in golf; it was the biggest and will always be the biggest."

Chapter 6

JONES MEETS A KINDRED SOUL IN HOGAN

WHILE HE WAS ON TOUR with Valerie in 1938, Hogan received an invitation to play in the Masters Tournament in Augusta, Georgia. He was surprised because at the time Bobby Jones personally issued the Masters invitations using criteria known only to Jones himself. Even under the current qualifying rules, Ben still wouldn't have been invited. Ben was a nobody. How had Jones heard of him?

Ben's anxiety grew as he pulled the car off Washington Road and headed down Magnolia Drive to the course. Both Ben and Valerie were moved by the sight of the beautiful magnolia trees, the Spanish moss spreading to form an arch across the road as though it were welcoming conquering heroes.

Ben was hardly a conquering hero, yet. But his friend Byron Nelson was: He had won the Masters the year before. To Ben, it was more proof of how far behind he had fallen, and he felt even more overwhelmed at his arrival into such august company.

"Do you think we'll see Bobby Jones?" Valerie asked as they got out of the car.

"I don't know, Val. It takes a lot of work to run a golf tournament. I imagine he'll be too busy to worry about us."

As he spoke, Ben hurried in the direction of the end of the clubhouse to peek at the course.

"I'm really looking forward to seeing the course. After that driveway and this beautiful old clubhouse, I just can't wait any longer." Ben stuck his hand out for Val to join him.

Val ran to catch up, and the course came into view. It was lush and green, and they walked into the shade of a big live oak tree behind the clubhouse.

"You can see almost all of the holes from right here," Ben whispered.

"Good!" Valerie nodded in agreement. "That means I'll be able to watch you practice this time." Valerie never followed Ben around the course when he played because she didn't want to add to his nervousness.

Ben headed for the practice range while his caddy retrieved his bag. As he did, he sensed someone watching him.

"Aren't you Ben Hogan?" a voice asked.

Turning around, Ben found himself looking into the face he had memorized from the Movietone newsreels.

"Well, yes, I am, Mr. Jones," Ben said. "Thank you for inviting me to play." It happened so fast Ben had not had time to get nervous, and he extended his hand to shake the outstretched one of Bobby Jones.

"We hope you'll enjoy your stay and the course, Ben. How did you finish up in Jacksonville? I've been so busy getting things ready for this tournament, I haven't had time to hear the results." Jones was gracious and attentive.

"Craig Wood won it with a final round of 69. No one else was really in it at the end," Ben offered.

"Good, Craig needed a win. Who shot the low round of the week?" Jones put his hand on Ben's shoulder as they walked down the hill.

"I did, Mr. Jones. A 67 in the third round."

"A 67 on that course is a commendable score. Congratulations."

"Thank you, Mr. Jones. It was one of my better efforts."

"Please call me Bob. My fans called me Bobby, but my friends know me as Bob."

Ben almost lost his breath. Not only had Jones invited him to play in his hallowed Masters Tournament, he had complimented him on his game, and now he had called Ben a friend. For a moment, Ben didn't think life could get any better.

"Ben, I hear you set standards for practicing on tour. The other pros tell me you practice more than anyone else."

"Well, I do seem to be out there a lot by myself." Ben grew uncomfortable being in the spotlight. His game wasn't all that great. Hell, I just started winning money, he thought.

To move the conversation away from himself, Ben said, "I've heard you hardly ever practiced when you were competing."

"For reasons of their own, some people like to think the

game came very easily to me. In fact, I spent many, many hours practicing off the 8th fairway at East Lake, where Stewart Maiden, the pro there, sent me. He often told me to stay out until I learned how to hit this shot or that shot. As a young man I looked up to Stewart and lived by his word. Still do."

"I'd like to play East Lake myself someday to see where you started."

"Why, thank you, Ben." Jones looked surprised, and Ben marveled at the grace of a man who could be flattered by such a small comment.

Jones began again. "I'm sure Stewart will treat you right and see to it that you get a good caddy. By the way, your caddy this week is Cheeks, and he's very good except for one thing. He sometimes neglects to consider the effect of grain on the putts." Jones smiled.

"Thank you sir . . . er, Bob. I certainly won't forget about that."

"It's been nice making your acquaintance, Ben. I hope I'll see you again. I've got a little problem with the 12th green that I must look at now. Because of the shade, it's always about a month behind the other greens. Someday we'll figure out a way to warm it up without cutting down another beautiful old tree."

With that, Jones took off at a fast clip, and Ben had one of his best practice sessions. He hit shot after shot right on target and, as he did, he discovered one of the master's wry secrets.

Ben's caddy, Cheeks, acquired his nickname from Jones. As he chased Ben's balls, Ben found out why. He had the fattest cheeks Ben had ever seen, and even from a distance,

Ben could see them bouncing. The sight kept Ben laughing through the long practice session.

It wasn't the first secret he shared with Jones, but it was the first one Ben knew about.

Seeing Valerie under the big tree behind the clubhouse, Ben said, "You missed all the action."

"I saw how your shots all landed on target," she preened.

"Not that action. Something more important. I met the man we've been watching on the screen at your father's movie house."

Valerie was stunned. "You mean you've already met Bobby Jones?"

"He wants to be called Bob by you and me," Ben said proudly. "Wait until you meet him. He's just like the guy we saw in the movies. There's nothing fake about him. He's just about the most polite guy I've ever met."

"Oh, Val," Ben's words came out in a torrent. "He has this aura around him. You can really feel his presence."

Just then, a man came down from the clubhouse and asked Ben to play a round of golf with Mr. Jones, at Ben's convenience.

Ben was taken aback. He himself had never asked other golfers to have a game with him. They had their own friends and their own circles of partners. Ben usually played alone. Now, here was the great Bobby Jones asking him for a game. What on earth was happening?

"I'd be pleased to play with Mr. Jones anytime he wishes," Ben replied, and the messenger suggested a noon tee-off.

With Valerie watching from under her adopted tree, Ben and Jones teed off a few hours later. Ben had spent the intervening time, as usual, on the practice range.

"Since you're a guest here, Ben, you have the honors."

Ben's hands shook as he teed up his ball, and he was ashamed at the tremor.

As they started down the fairway, Jones again mentioned Ben's devotion to practice. "You've already put in more time on our practice tee than Hagen has in the three years he's played here."

"I have?"

"Yes. Walter practices at a course over in South Carolina. I believe he doesn't want us to know how much he practices. He probably thinks it would hurt his image. He doesn't know a few of our members are locals who live on that course. Walter has so many ploys he sometimes has a hard time keeping up with them." Jones laughed, easing Ben's tension.

"You have to understand how important image is to Walter," Jones continued. "Sarazen knows him in and out, though. Gene can tell you everything about him. Walter hasn't been able to put anything over on Gene since that tie from the blonde trick in the '23 PGA Championship."

Joining in the banter, Ben said, "What was the truth about that?"

"Well, Walter was trying to throw Gene off his game, so he sent a boxed tie to his motel room the night prior to the match with a note from an anonymous blonde. The note said she'd be waiting for him in the gallery the final day and invited him to wear the tie just for her. It worked for a while. Dressed up in his tie, Gene spent a good deal of time looking for his secret admirer. Walter gave it away by laughing, and Gene finally figured out who sent the tie. Gene won anyway on the second playoff hole."

Ben's approach shot on the 1st hole was perfect, and he and Jones shot matched pars.

Ben still had the honors on the 2nd hole, and his drive flew over the sole fairway bunker and drew back down the fairway. Jones's draw was smoothly played and it hugged the treeline on the left before alighting on a spot in the middle of the fairway.

Walking off the tee, Jones said, "I see you lost your shaky hand on that tee."

"It's not something I'm proud of." Ben's face grew hot.

"Ben, if I had a birdie for every time my hands shook, I'd have rewritten all the record books at the age of twenty-five. All a shaky hand does is show how much something really means to you."

"It feels like weakness to me," Ben stammered.

"Ben, my hardest matches were always against players whose hands shook. It showed how badly they wanted it. Guys whose hands don't shake don't care. Of course, some people have a difficult time showing their feelings, Ben. Some people shake only on the inside, like Hagen."

What an extraordinary day, Ben thought. How did I get so lucky all of a sudden?

Jones's approach was short and Ben's pulled up left and short. As they both pitched on and two-putted for pars, Jones impressed Ben by thanking his caddy for his help on the hole. Thanking your caddy for helping you on the course you built must be the ace of sportsmanship, Ben thought.

On the 3rd hole, both golfers hit spoons, which landed in the middle of the fairway.

Ben's nine-iron approach bit, but rolled to the back. Jones punched a little eight-iron that bounced onto the putting surface, rolled toward the pin, and then curled left. Two more pars.

"Now this is what I call a friendly game, Ben. The course is holding its own against both of us. No birdies and no bogies."

"Don't worry, I've heard the next two holes are going to test our status," Ben replied. "The guy who laid them out knew what he was doing after allowing those warm-up holes," Ben chuckled, enjoying the first joke he had ever told on a golf course.

"Wait until Thursday to see if you consider the 1st hole a warm-up. Every year, the 1st hole climbs in scoring average as the tournament seems to grow in meaning. I don't expect this year to be any different."

As they walked, Jones pointed out how he would play each hole. He showed Ben the best side from which to approach each green, a tip all players struggled to find. Jones even recommended that Ben walk the course backwards during a practice round to further grasp the nature of the course. Jones said it would tell him more about the course than anything else.

On the 4th hole, Ben hit a three-iron that reached into the middle of the green while Bob cut a two-iron that floated onto the surface and bit.

"Bob, is it true that you lost a lot of weight while competing for the four majors in 1930?"

"I lost a lot of weight competing prior to 1929," Jones replied. "After 1929, I lost little or no weight, however. At least, it seemed to stay on a lot easier," Jones chuckled.

"My wife Val was worried it might happen to me."

"Once you reach a certain level of acceptance playing

the majors, Ben, you'll find an inner peace that makes it easier to perform."

Ben smiled at Jones, silently thanking him for his help. It was as if Jones was turning all his knowledge over to Ben, and no words could ever contain enough gratitude for such a gift.

Ben's drive on the long 5th hole started out in the middle, but drew back into the left edge. Jones hit a long draw that bounced into the right side.

There was a question burning inside Ben, and as they walked down the fairway, he got up the nerve to ask it. "Bob, do you think it's possible to build a swing that repeats itself every time, that can hold up under all conditions?"

"My own beliefs would say that if you're capable enough to think of it, you're capable enough to do it. I don't think anyone has ever tried to develop such a repetitive swing, although some of my competitors at times seemed to possess it," Jones smiled.

"That's what I hope to do," Ben admitted. "Build a swing that repeats like it's automatic. At times I already feel as though I've hit on it, only to find out what I'm doing isn't quite right yet because it won't hold up during a tournament."

"So that's why you're doing so much practicing."

"I really enjoy hitting balls, too." Ben smiled. "There's a special challenge in being able to make a ball do exactly what you want it to do, time after time, whether on a course or on a practice area. But, yes, I'm also working on building a repeating swing. A swing I can repeat under any and all situations, even when my nerves are being jangled."

"That's the biggest challenge, isn't it," Jones said as

though he was reading Ben's mind. "To measure up to the challenge of playing well in front of thousands of people, to please them."

Ben lowered his gaze, embarrassed by his desire to please others.

Jones stepped forward to let Ben know they weren't so different after all. "That's why I lost the weight, Ben. I was afraid I wouldn't be able to live up to the expectations people had of me. It's easy to create a good stroke in practice. Taking it to the first tee in a tournament is the challenge. And taking it to the first tee in a major is its own hell."

"This first major tournament is just practice for me," Ben said. "No one knows I'm alive yet."

"It was that way for me too, at first. Of course, that's not how it turned out." Unlike Ben, Jones had always been a winner.

After they both putted out for pars on the 5th hole, Jones laughed and said, "Maybe we're just meant to play even up all the way around. That would be an unusual occurrence on this course."

"I don't think that's going to happen," Ben said, taking the quiet challenge Jones had issued. "We're just starting out friendly," and he grinned at the new friend who had made him feel welcome for the first time in his life.

Ben's six-iron on the short 6th hit short of the pin, bounced past the hole, and then drew back.

"Nice," Bob said.

"Thanks," Ben replied in a soft and humble voice, while thinking to himself, "finally."

Jones's six-iron faded in on target, hit left of the cup, rolled past the pin, and curled slightly down.

"Now that's some golf," Jones enthusiastically exclaimed as the two of them started down the steep hill, the gravity of the slope forcing bigger steps.

Jones's putt firmly entered the cup while Ben's putt rimmed it on the lower side. Jones conceded Ben's putt, and the gracious control Jones exhibited in the gesture gave Ben a premonition that he was going to put on a display.

On the 7th hole, Jones ripped a drive, while Ben's horrendous hook shot through the trees on the left and wound up on the third fairway.

"I heard you had a penchant for hitting those," Jones said to a downcast Ben.

"It's my worst nightmare. Sarazen says even Walter Hagen would have a tough time playing back from one of my hooks."

"Ben, no one has it easy. Everyone has his own unique set of problems to overcome. This is simply one of yours. You'll win the battle one day. I still have quite a few to win over."

Ben was struck by the openness and honesty of Jones's comment. So Bobby Jones had things to overcome, too. Ben had always believed the game came easily to Jones.

Ben played his recovery shot safely out to the middle of the fairway and then he pitched on, as Jones had already done.

After Ben two-putted, backhanding in his little second putt, Jones knocked in an eight-footer to continue his run.

With the honors still in hand, Jones uncorked another long drive on the 8th hole. Ben tentatively hit his drive which, because of his cautiousness, hooked but not as wildly as before. Ben felt beaten. Here he was, playing with Bobby

Jones, and he couldn't even get off the tee properly.

"In the old days, if I were you, Ben, clubs would have filled the air by now. I'm sorry you're not doing what you're so obviously capable of." It was as though Jones saw into Ben's heart and, liking what he saw, wanted to offer comfort.

"If only I never again had to fear a hook," Ben said.

"That's possible for you, Ben. The first step toward accomplishment is believing. That makes the other steps come easier and faster."

It just couldn't be that easy, Ben thought. As they walked on in silence, Ben swore he could feel Jones pulling for him. It filled him with the warmth he usually got only from Valerie.

Ben hit his next shot back to the fairway and proceeded to rip a spoon from a tight lie all the way up the right side. It bounced through the bunker surrounding the green. Jones's spoon went straight for the green.

"Great shot, Bob. Nicely done," Ben offered, now filled with enthusiasm for the game.

"Thanks, Ben. Well, everything they told me about you has been right on the money except for a few little things."

Ben couldn't understand how he had attracted the attention of the immortal Bobby Jones, and he could only offer an "Oh."

"They underestimate how much heart you have," Jones continued. "As soon as you control that hook and start believing in yourself, you're going to become someone impressive. You make me glad I retired. Now I don't have to worry about guys like you coming along to beat my best game anymore." Bob was smiling as he walked, gazing up at the sky.

"At times," Ben tried to downplay the compliment, "I feel so beaten by my hook. It's my worst problem. Right behind that is playing in front of all the people. It's so hard for me to concentrate once they both start to get to me." Ben's eyes were riveted to the ground.

"Ben." Jones was solemn. "You fought your way back on tour after failure and still had the fortitude to go on despite continued losses. You have my respect."

Jones's words of praise lifted Ben out of his malaise and gave him hope.

They finished out the 8th hole with Jones gaining another stroke and then walked to the 9th tee. Ben had fallen three strokes behind Jones, but he wasn't about to quit.

Jones's fine drive was followed by Ben's best of the day, which rolled well past Jones's. Jones's approach was long but drew back while Ben's was shy of the cup, leaving him a short uphill putt.

After he missed his fifteen-foot putt, Jones walked around behind Ben. "Knock it in," Jones encouraged. Ben did and Jones followed.

As they were walking to the 10th tee, someone came running down to them from the clubhouse. "Oh no," Jones said. "I hope they're not going to cut this round short." Ben watched as Cliff Roberts, Jones's partner at Augusta National, came into view.

"Wait for me," Jones said. "I'll be gone for only a few minutes."

Jones returned with a smile on his face. "It wasn't as bad as I thought. They don't need me half as much as they like to believe they do. They just want to make sure I feel wanted." Jones was now looking down the 10th fairway.

"It's nice of them to care," Ben added as he spotted Valerie watching from under the tree. He was happy to have the honors so that he could show off to her. Ben's draw played the fairway perfectly. Jones followed suit.

"How did you overcome most of the problems you encountered playing major tournament golf?" Ben asked, hoping to get some practical advice.

The question transported Jones into his memories, and he took awhile to answer it. "O.B. Keeler helped me work out most of my mental problems. We just walked and talked late at night and even early in the mornings before a tournament. I don't know when he found time to write his columns. He gave me all the time I needed. For that I'll always be very grateful to him."

"Do you think you could have worked your problems out alone?"

"Well, every man likes to think he can solve his problem alone, and maybe I could have. But I was very glad to have O.B.'s help. He was a great sounding board, and he brought a maturity and a wisdom to our conversations that I needed. In many ways, he is still a second father to me."

Their second shots to the 430-yard 10th hole were both close to the pin, and Jones quickly pointed out that the hole was due to be lengthened to 470 yards to toughen it up.

After their par putts rolled in, Ben asked, "Do you have any regrets about giving up the chase for championships?"

"Not on most days. But occasionally I miss the appreciative response of the crowd, or saying hello to people you meet only in tournaments." Jones walked onto the 11th tee, deep in thought. "Yes, I also miss being in the final round with a chance to prove myself once again. It can be very euphoric to have the acclaim of the fans, very euphoric.

"The problem with acclaim," Jones added, "is that it is addictive. Yes," he said with a tone bordering on awe. "It can be very habit-forming."

Their drives were slightly drawn, their steps a little lighter, and when they left the 11th tee they walked in unison.

It was a quiet time, a silent communication between the two men. From time to time, Jones talked about his dreams for the course and his tournament.

"Nothing worth doing well was ever done in a short time, Ben. Mother Nature encourages us to take our time and to slowly develop what we want. No matter what we want to accomplish, quality takes time."

"Well, I like the course the way it already is," Ben replied. "It has a serenity that sets it apart from other courses. Almost as though it challenges you to learn its intricacies and conquer its secrets."

"That's what golf is all about, Ben. Enjoying the intricacies of the game and the personal inner challenge that confronts us on each and every shot. When you start challenging for your majors, Ben, find your love of the game. It's what will carry you to where you want to go." Jones caught Ben in his gaze. "There are only two forces in the world, Ben, love and fear."

It would be a long time before Ben understood what Jones really meant. For now, there were more lessons.

Jones and Ben completed their pars on the 11th hole.

"Now we get to play my favorite hole and see how my changes to her are coming along."

"I'm glad you're going first," Ben replied. "The designer of this hole must have been working off a bad night's sleep."

"I'd agree with you, Ben, but the main designer of this little beauty was Alister McKenzie. It's similar to one of the holes he used to play over in the British Isles. A testy little jewel that teaches you what this game is all about. You can measure it off or you can try to feel it, but finally you must simply trust yourself to do well, or suffer the consequences.

Jones looked back at the movement of the flag on the 11th green and forward to the trees behind the 12th hole. He faded a six-iron onto the left side of the green, as did Ben, following his mentor. They both made long putts for birdies.

"Here's our reward for getting past the 12th so well," Jones said as he teed up on the 13th hole." This hole plays easily for the player who made a par on 12. There's less pressure to it. But it is harder for the player who has to get a birdie to make up for his mistake."

Jones's drive on 13 faded out to the right, and Ben hit a draw that cut the corner perfectly.

"Did traveling with your wife help you this time out, Ben?"

"It was the difference between a 76 and a 71," Ben said. "Val helped me the way you said O.B. Keeler helped you. I don't think I would have made it without her."

"Isn't it funny, Ben? People keep wanting to believe we do these things alone. I doubt there's a good golfer alive who would take the sole credit for what he's accomplished. Except for Walter, of course." Jones laughed so loud, other golfers heard him on the next fairway and wondered what he was doing with Ben Hogan.

Jones laid up short while Ben lashed a three-iron into the heart of the green. Jones chipped on and they both two-putted.

"Nice bird," Jones said to Ben.

"Thanks," Ben said in the hushed way that would become his custom when receiving a compliment on his game.

After their drives on the 14th hole, Jones asked Ben, "How many tournaments would you like to win to make you happy?"

"One," Ben quickly shot back. "This one." Jones's laugh showed how much he enjoyed Ben's answer, and he walked on in silence with a slight smile on his face.

"Your life will change after you win your first Masters. The spell of winning in front of the patrons will propel you. It is intoxicating to have their respect and admiration. They hang on your every movement, and the feeling is very powerful."

Ben's five-iron bounced before the green and rolled up the rise to within six feet of the hole. "I can see you don't need my help anymore. Nice shot," Jones said.

Ben shook his head slightly, "I hit it thin, but got lucky on the bounce. It's the first break I've had all day."

Jones's five-iron hit into the side of the rise and shot off to the back of the green. "Local knowledge," he said dryly.

Jones got down in two and watched Ben drop his slightly sidehill breaker. "Two breaks in a row. I'd like to keep this streak going for the next few days," Ben said in a rare positive comment about his game.

Both of their drives found the middle of the fairway on the 15th hole at the crest. Following Jones's lead, Ben laid his second shot up short. Jones pointed to the spot where Gene Sarazen had sunk his famous double eagle just three years before. "One in a thousand," Ben said, looking the shot over.

"Especially when you're playing with Walter and he's got a heavy date he's edgy to get to," Jones bantered back.

Both men hit wedges that ran over the hole, and they were left with tedious downhill putts. Jones missed his, but Ben's went in.

"Good playing, Ben."

"Thanks." Ben's seven-iron to the short 145-yard 16th bit and came back towards the little creek that guarded the front edge. Jones's seven-iron did not bite, and it rolled close to the pin. For the first time that day, Ben took three putts to get home while Jones curled his in.

Before they left the 16th green, Jones asked, "What would you think of this hole if it were moved back up on that bank? Then we could damn up this little creek to create some excitement for the approach shot."

"How long would the required shot be?" Ben asked.

"It would probably stretch from about 170 to about 190 yards."

"Definitely would make the finish more interesting with a test like that," Ben summed up as they started for the 17th tee. "You sound like you've still got a lot of refining to do on the course."

"Like life, this golf course will never stop changing, Ben. We get things just as we want them, and then the process starts all over again."

Jones's drive on the 17th hole was long and straight, while Ben, trying to show off a bit, hit one of his hard hooks that wound up off the back of the 7th green.

"Oh God, not you again," Ben bleated, referring to his hook. Jones saw the pain in Ben's eyes and felt sorry for him. We all have to find our own way, he thought.

Ben, relentless as ever, looked for an opportunity. He found that he still had a shot to the green by hitting it over the trees. Using his seven-iron, his shot cleared the trees before landing between the two traps guarding the green and bounding onto the green.

Jones's six-iron went through the green to the fringe on the back. His chip back was too hard, though, and it rolled strongly past the cup. Jones's frustration was evident from across the green, and Ben didn't feel so alone.

They both two-putted and walked to the final tee, where they were met by Cliff Roberts and his friend, Bobby Austin.

"Did you come out to make sure I made it in, Cliff?" Bob joked.

"No, I came out to give you some help," Roberts joked back. "Actually, I came out to cheer you two on," and he looked at Ben to see what he was made of. He had never seen Jones give so much time to an untalented rookie.

Ben's drive went left again, but not too badly, and afterward, Cliff spurred Jones on to split the fairway, which he did.

The four men walked off the tee in step. On his second shot, Ben's five-iron landed on the left side of the green and stayed there while Jones struck a six-iron right at the flag.

"Who's up?" Cliff asked.

"He is." Ben and Jones said in unison, sharing a laugh

only they understood.

"Friendly match," Cliff remarked dryly, joining his hands behind his back before watching Ben stroke his putt.

Ben's putt stopped on the edge and waited for him to nudge the little ball home.

"For you, Cliff," Bob teased as he lined up his shot and then sank his testy sidehiller.

Much to Cliff Robert's surprise, Jones asked Ben for another game. "Can we do this again tomorrow, Ben? I've enjoyed our round more than any other in a long time." Jones laid his hand on Ben's shoulder, and Ben felt its power and warmth.

Under Cliff Roberts's scrutinizing stare, Ben merely grunted his thanks.

Valerie joined Ben as the men parted company. "Did you beat 65?" Valerie asked, thinking back to Ben's best round so far on the tour.

"I shot a 70. But the score was incidental to what really happened out there. Playing with Jones has lifted me to a new place in my game. I feel like I can play with anyone now."

"That's probably why he did it."

"Did what, Val?"

"That's probably why he played with you."

"To elevate my game?"

"Things don't just happen by coincidence, Ben."

"Why would he bother with me? I'm just a nobody."

"Maybe he sees what I do."

The next day, Ben was surprised when Jones's caddy set up another game. He had thought Jones's offer of a second round was merely a polite gesture. He was wrong.

This time, Ben decided to pick up pointers from Jones about his swing or the shots he chose to play. Jones never talked about these things, and Ben sensed there was a secret to be learned from his silence.

"Do you notice anything I could be doing better?" Ben asked.

"There's always something we could be doing better, Ben. That's the beautiful part of this game. You have a fine game and a fine swing to build on."

"But is my swing good enough as it is? Maybe I should get it a little more upright?" Ben asked, doggedly pursuing his goal.

"If you're closing in on your goals, Ben, your swing is good enough." Jones knew he wasn't giving Ben what he wanted.

"Ben, most people think that challenges come from the outside. You are different. It's been obvious to me for a while now that you're the type of person who is always reaching inside to face the ultimate challenge. Facing up to that inner challenge will carry you to the victories I know you're already very capable of achieving."

As they finished their round, Valerie was waiting for Ben. "How'd it go?" Valerie asked excitedly.

"Well, the round was great, but Jones didn't talk about the things I expected him to." Ben looked perplexed.

"What were you expecting?"

"Tips about fixing my hook or how to perfect my swing."

"Well, what did Jones tell you?"

Ben and Valerie strolled toward the practice range,

past the majestic clubhouse, under the magnolia trees on the front lawn. Ben was silent, trying to digest his mystical conversations with Jones.

"Val, he told me that I should be winning now. He told me I'm already capable of winning tournaments."

"I've told you that myself, Ben What else did he talk about?"

"Well, he talked a lot of about fear and love."

Chapter 7

THE SPORTSWRITERS ALMOST RUIN HOGAN'S GAME

BEN DIDN'T PERFORM VERY WELL in his first Masters Tournament. However, while the Masters would wait for Ben to come to it, the sportswriters would not.

In the weeks following the Masters, as Ben played in the Cotton Classic, then in the Azalea Open, and finally at the North and South Open in Pinehurst, his game began to improve dramatically. He wasn't able to put his finger on what had caused the change, but there was a change nonetheless.

Facts are fact, he thought as he looked at his scores. He was now averaging almost one and a half strokes better in each seventy-two-hole tournament. It had been the fastest and most dramatic improvement in his game since he had begun recording changes in his little black books, and it had occurred right after he played with Bobby Jones.

Maybe that repetitive swing is finally starting to kick in, he thought, always looking for a mechanical reason for his success.

Ben's rise up the leader board also became visible to the people who followed the growing tournament trail. Toney Penna made Ben an offer to join MacGregor as a representative of their clubs on tour, and Ben gladly accepted. It meant a thousand dollars and one free set of golf clubs each year, plus a dozen free balls for every tournament. Most of all, because Penna, Byron Nelson, Jimmy Demaret, and Lloyd Mangrum were already MacGregor representatives, Ben's acceptance into their elite circle sent his spirits soaring.

Unfortunately, Ben's success also telegraphed his name to the sportswriters, who were looking for a talkative new star to fill their columns with the "golf secrets" of the day.

Golf "secrets" were becoming hot commodities with sportswriters, pros, and fans alike. In part, this was because as more and more golfers joined the pro tour, so too grew the number of players to beat. Thus, the pros searched constantly for new ways to improve their game, for golfing secrets. Shaving just one stroke per round often meant survival, a chance to stay on the tour in an era of small purses that paid through only twelve or fifteen places.

The competition for secrets grew fierce. Whenever one golfer found a way to improve his score, the other golfers were quick to discover it. A pro who made a small change in any part of his swing, his stance, or his grip, set off a chain reaction through the ranks. Other golfers either incorporated the change or discarded it on the heap of yesterday's secrets.

Talk about secrets among the pros became a contagious disease and dominated their interactions. "Have you tried Snead's new grip?" "What do you think of Nelson's knee dip?"

Unfortunately, the sportswriters were infected by the disease almost as quickly as the pros. Fans all across America were eager to improve their games and copy editors demanded more secrets from their writers. "That last article on Snead's new grip was great. I picked up a club and tried holding it as I would a small bird, just like Snead recommended. It worked! Dig up a few more secrets like that for today's deadline."

At first, Ben was no different from the other pros and was often on the lookout for playing tips. He had learned so much from watching Bobby Jones's instructional films, he thought he could also pick up little things from others.

On more than a few occasions, he saw Tommy Armour, Walter Hagen, or Craig Wood do something different and then tried to incorporate the change into his repetitive swing during practice. These innovations often were simple things, but they could also amount to a whole swing change, from the flat swing of Hagen to the upright swing of Tommy Armour.

However, after trying hundreds of variations, Ben decided he was better off digging ideas out on his own. Nothing he ever borrowed from anyone else stayed in his swing. He just couldn't make the changes work when the stakes were raised. Although he wouldn't realize it for a few years yet, it wasn't the mechanical part of the game that defeated Ben in the final round.

Try as he might, Ben's game could not stand up to the scrutiny of the fans. With no ropes to hold people away from the players, fans walked right down the fairway with their favorite pros and breathed down their necks as they putted. No amount of practice gave Ben the tough gallery nerves he needed. And although Valerie's mental tricks helped, he simply could not keep fans from interfering with his game.

Consequently, at the North and South Open, Ben faltered on the fourth round and shot a 78. He was ready to grab his bags and disappear when Jasper Walters of United Press International grabbed him.

"How about a few minutes so that your fans can hear from you?"

"Okay," Ben said, with a hesitation to his voice. He didn't understand why anyone would want details on how he lost a tournament, but he agreed to the interview for Valerie's sake. Valerie wanted Ben to become friendlier with fans. She thought they would respect his playing privacy if they knew him better.

"Ben, from watching your scores, it's obvious you're gaining on the tour. How about giving your fans a nice story on how you do it."

"What would you like, Jasper?"

"Oh, you know, Ben, give us the kind of stories we get from Sarazan and Wood. You know, the secrets they all say you're discovering out in the practice area."

"I wish I could help you, but I'm not keeping any secrets. If I had any secrets, they wouldn't stay secrets very long. I play in front of thousands of people every week."

"But you must have some little tip everyone would gain from knowing."

"Well, I guess everyone who plays golf could use more practice."

"You mean you're not going to tell us your secrets?"

"I don't think there are any secrets to this game, Jasper. You just keep hitting the ball closer to the hole until it goes in."

Walters's UPI article led newspapers the next day with the headline, TEXAS TERMITE REFUSES TO HELP HIS FANS.

From that moment on, Ben was the golfer sportswriters wanted to trap into an interview. His innocence, his unabashed honesty, when set in cold black print, without emotion, made great copy.

At the St. Petersburg Open, Ben was only two strokes off the lead going into the 70th hole. It was his first real chance to win a tournament.

On the 71st tee, Ben hooked his drive and punched himself out of the running. As he was walking off the course, head down in disgust, a sportswriter for the *St. Petersburg Star* cornered him.

"Tell me how it feels to have been so close and lose out on the last couple of holes."

"You wouldn't want to print that, Bill," Ben said, shaking his head.

"Well, then, tell us what you're going to do differently next time you get a chance to win."

"If I knew that, I would have won today instead of coming in second."

"Well, how about giving something of value to all the golfers who follow your name on the sports page?"

"Just like in other sports, Bill, practice is an intimate part of the game. The more you practice, the better you play. A lot of people don't think pros need practice, but we do. In fact, judging by today's play, some of us need to practice more."

"That's it? Practice?"

The *St. Petersburg Star* ran this headline the next morning, MR. RUNNER-UP THINKS HIS COMPETITION SHOULD PRACTICE MORE.

The Mr. Runner-up label stuck to Ben in print and on the course as the first-place spot eluded him in tournament after tournament.

Soon, the New York sports pages reported that Ben must have figured a new way to finish out of the running, because he had pretty much worn out all the old ways.

"They just twist my words to sell more papers," Ben complained to Valerie after another second-place finish.

At the 1939 Masters, Ben opened with a round of 75. By concentrating hard, he followed the 75 with a 71, then two 72s, and finished in ninth position. Another pro might have been happy seeing his name on the Augusta leader board for the first time, but not Ben. His efforts didn't produce the win he wanted so badly on the course that Jones had built.

One sportswriter recommended that the Mr. Runner-up title be awarded to Ben permanently.

Christmas at the Hogan house in Fort Worth that year was a heavy and somber time.

"I don't know how much more time and effort I can put

into the tour without winning, Val," Ben said, warming his hands with a cup of black coffee.

"You have a lot to be proud of, Ben."

"But unless I can win, I haven't accomplished what I set out to do. I can't be known as Mr. Runner-up forever, Val. I've dragged you all over this country and haven't been able to deliver on my promises, either to you or myself. I hate that I've let you down."

"You haven't let me down, Ben, not for one minute," Val said as she went to Ben's side, offering her strength in place of his own. "You're the winner I always knew you were. The only person who doesn't believe it is you."

"Yeah, me and the sportswriters. When I see Nelson and Guldahl and Demaret winning – Snead, too, and right off the bat – I wonder what's wrong with me. I beat all these guys in practice, and when a tournament starts, they leave me behind like an old hickory shaft."

"I hate to see you this low, Ben."

He sighed. "I guess for my own sake, I need to put a limit on my time left on tour. If I don't win by a certain date, I need to accept the fact that there must be something better for me to do."

"You mean you'd give up this game you love so much? I didn't think I'd ever hear you say that."

"It's time, Val. I don't think I can take much more of this."

"All right, then. What kind of time limit do you have in mind? You certainly don't need to put any more pressure on yourself with a deadline that's too short."

"Well, we've been at this for almost four years. I just can't see going past another year. I've come close enough times that I should be able to win this next year. If I don't, I'll feel like I've tried hard enough. No one can take being a runner-up forever."

Ben's first opportunity to achieve his goal during the 1940 tour took place in Oakland, California. It was the same tournament that had saved Ben once before, two years earlier when he and Valerie were out of money. His $385 check had kept them on the tour.

Perhaps more importantly, the tournament had taught Ben to look past his own psyche for victory. That day, Ben had had to do more than jump into the top ten to place in the money. He had had to overlook the rage building inside him after discovering his tires had been stolen.

That day, despite all obstacles, Ben had achieved his goal. Today, he remembered this well and put almost as much pressure on himself, wondering if he would be able to do it again.

Ben started out the Oakland tournament with a 73 and followed with a 72. His game was steady, but he knew pars did not win tournaments.

Frustrated, he practiced hard the morning of the third round. "I've just got to make my move," he thought as he methodically hit his practice balls. Ben trailed Clayton Heafner, who had just come onto the tour from North Carolina, by four strokes.

In the third round, Ben fought back, shooting a 68. He now trailed Heafner by just two shots.

Still not pleased with his progress, Ben complained to Valerie over dinner that night.

"Would you believe he was a candymaker in North Carolina before coming on tour? It seems anyone can show up and win except me," Ben groaned. "A candymaker! Of all things."

"You're too hard on yourself. You'll win soon, I know you will. Besides, Heafner hasn't won anything yet."

"He's going to win his first time out. Just you wait and see. Maybe there's a message for me in all this." Ben shook his head, scowling into his coffee.

"Your time will come. Take some of the pressure off yourself, please. You'll win, Ben. You'll win. When you do, you'll appreciate it more because of how hard you worked to earn it."

Ben's fourth round was another close one. He scraped for each score and finished just after noon, joining Valerie at the scorer's table to wait for the finish.

"We've got a great chance, Val," Ben said as he checked over his scorecard. "This should be a 69 if my hopes haven't clouded the score."

Byron Nelson's wife, Louise, walked by the table and gave Valerie a thumbs-up, signifying her hope that Ben had won the tournament.

"Yep, it's a 69," Ben said as he verified his score. "Total for the four rounds is 282. Let him try to match that."

"Whatever happens, you did your best, Ben. Let's go have some lunch."

While they were eating, Byron Nelson, Horton Smith, and Vic Ghezzi passed Ben's table to congratulate him on his leading score.

"What's your final, Ben? 282? That should take it. Congratulations," Ghezzi said as he passed Ben.

"Thanks, Vic. See you next week in San Francisco,"

Ben returned.

Ben and Valerie finished lunch and packed their bags to fill the time before returning to the tournament and their fate.

Standing at the back of the 18th green, Ben heard Heafner had had trouble on the 16th hole and would have to birdie at least one of the last two holes to tie Ben's score of 282.

Ben turned to smile at Valerie and heard a cheer coming from the fans surrounding the 17th green. He wasn't sure which player had earned applause, but it worried him.

As Heafner walked up to tee off first on the 18th hole, Ben knew the cheer had been for Heafner.

Heafner put his second shot onto the green of the par four 18th, and Ben asked a nearby caddy for an update. Heafner had birdied 17. That meant Ben and Heafner were tied for the tournament at six under.

"Maybe we shouldn't have packed," Ben said to Valerie, as he considered the possibility of a playoff the next day.

Heafner addressed his putt. Ben watched as the ball disappeared into the hole, giving Heafner the tournament at seven under.

As the fans roared in appreciation for Heafner's effort, Ben's heart pounded in his chest. The tournament had been taken right out of his hands. From first place to runner-up in a fraction of a second.

"You did well," Valerie said as she looked into Ben's tight, rigid face.

"Congratulations, Clayt," Ben called out to the winner as he walked off the 18th green.

"Thanks, Ben. I feel like I've been through it. I was really lucky out there," Heafner offered back.

In the parking lot, Nelson walked past Ben and Valerie as they were packing their car.

"Sorry, Ben," he said.

"Thanks, Byron," Ben returned.

"On to Frisco," Ben said dryly, climbing into the car and slamming the door.

In San Francisco, the tournament would be match play. Players competed for each individual hole rather than keeping a running score. A match-play tournament was always a popular event because it broke up the monotony of weekly stroke play.

Even though Ben qualified for the tournament by just one stroke, he hoped for an early win over his first opponent, a newcomer named Porky Oliver.

It was a close match, as neither man pulled away from the other. One hole up, and then they were even. One hole down, and even again. Oliver's long putts and great chips kept him in the game until the end and wore down Ben's resistance.

When Oliver won the 15th and 17th holes, Ben was beaten by two down with one to go.

His only comment at the end of the tournament was to Valerie. "Let's get out of here."

Ben was invited to play in the Bing Crosby Pro-Amateur, a thirty-six-hole event just outside San Diego, California. At the Bing Crosby, the pros were expected to partner with the stars. The bigger the star, the more important a player you became during the tournament. Naturally, it was popular with pros and fans who liked to mingle with

Crosby's movie star friends.

The presence of Hollywood stars whipped the galleries into a whirlwind, and the pros were mentally challenged to remember they were there to play golf. Ben was obviously no exception, so he devised a trick to stay focused.

Ben surprised them all by asking for a lesser-known star, hoping he would then be left alone to concentrate on his game.

In his first round, Ben shot a 71 and trailed the leader, Porky Oliver, by three strokes.

"Well, how did you feel out there today? Were you able to keep your concentration?" Valerie asked Ben as he joined her under the umbrellas for a bite to eat.

"As long as the crowds followed the other players, I was fine. Even the sportswriters ignored me today. They were busy bothering everyone else."

The following morning, Ben got up early and hit the practice area before the crowds arrived. The control he had exhibited the day before in the midst of chaos now translated into a perfect practice session, and his confidence soared.

"Maybe that's the secret," he thought, "finding a way to be ignored."

Ben stood at two under after the first nine holes. Struggling to ignore the wild war whoops coming from crowds on the other holes, Ben kept his eyes straight ahead. He knew he had a chance if Oliver faltered, if he could only keep his concentration. He muttered a silent mantra to himself as he walked along. "The course is empty. The course is empty."

Ben finished the round with a birdie on the 18th hole, then walked to the edge of the green and looked into the gallery for the first time. He was surprised to see Valerie standing there.

"How long have you been here?" Ben asked.

"All day," was her reply.

"I shot a 68."

"Yes, I know."

Ben turned in his score at the scorer's table and quickly went to Valerie's side.

"We have a chance. It's only thirty-six holes, but it would be a good one to win. Oliver will be finishing in about twenty minutes. I haven't heard anything about how he's doing."

"Oh, Ben." There was a heartbroken tone to Valerie's voice, and Ben's jaw tightened in response.

"What have I missed?" he said solemnly.

"Both he and Jug McSpaden are tearing up the course. Porky is actually one stroke better than the score you posted. I'm sorry," she said, hating to be the one to tell him. Ben was dumbstruck. No matter what he shot, he thought, someone would always shoot a better score to beat him.

In the end, Oliver won at 135 for the two rounds. Hogan was tied for second at 139.

Ben left the tournament so frustrated he could have driven to the next site in one long push, but he surprised Valerie by agreeing to a layover en-route to Phoenix.

"Let's try to enjoy the trip and have some fun," she said. "We got an early start on the rest of the guys."

"I've tried everything else," Ben replied. "Maybe they'll have a pool, and we can relax in the sun."

Ben arrived in Phoenix so rested, he was ready for his next charge up Hogan's hill.

Maybe Val is right, he thought. Maybe all this pressure messes up my game. It would give those high-and-mighty sportswriters a jolt to learn the secret is a good night's sleep.

But it wasn't Ben's secret.

He played well in Phoenix, tying for first, but he made a fatal error on the 15th hole of the playoff. His approach shot drew too much and caught the water on the left side of the green. He fought back, but in the end it was his own mistake that caused him to lose.

He was runner-up again at the next tournament, the Texas State Open.

"I should have won it, Val. It was my own state Open." Ben looked out into the distance when he said it, but Valerie could see the pain in his heart.

It was on to the North and South Open in Pinehurst, North Carolina, when Valerie suggested another diversion to try and lift Ben's spirits.

"How about stopping in to see Bobby Jones as we're driving past Augusta?"

"Hmpf." He grunted at the suggestion, but then, once again, surprised her by agreeing. "I could use another day of practice. Maybe Bob will let me use the driving range."

"We could both use a ride down Magnolia Lane."

"Well, it can't hurt. I just hope he hasn't heard about my performance on tour. I don't need to be reminded that I've let everyone down."

"Oh, Ben, you know how much Bob likes you. He'll be thrilled to see you, no matter what the circumstances."

As they parked the car in front of the manor house that would become the world-famous August National Clubhouse,

Ben spied Jones under a tree reading paperwork.

"What a place to get things done!" Ben said as he walked up to greet his only supporter in pro golf.

"Hey," Jones drawled. "God, it's good to see you two," and he stood up and held out his hand in a warm embrace.

"Can I getcha both a drink?"

"No thanks," Ben replied.

"Well, Ben, what's new?" Jones asked as they walked to the clubhouse and settled themselves into rocking chairs on the veranda overlooking the 18th green.

"Nothing," Ben grunted. "That's the trouble."

"Tell me about it."

"I either start strong and finish like a fool or start like a fool, come on strong, and finish short."

"I wouldn't have mentioned your recent scores for the world today, Ben. But since you brought it up, I have to know. What's eating at you?" Whether playing in a tournament or counseling his friends, Jones had a way of going right to the score.

"The same old things," Ben replied. "A hook that won't go away and sportswriters who want to pick on me."

"Ben, I'm going to tell you something you may not be ready to hear. You have to find a way to make your fear work for you."

"Fear! But I'm not afraid of a pack of double-dealing sportswriters."

Jones's voice dropped to a whisper, and Ben was forced to move forward in his chair to hear him. "It doesn't matter what you call it, Ben. Behind that anger of yours is fear."

"What do you think he meant by that?" Ben asked Valerie as they walked back to their car.

"I'm not quite sure, Ben. He seems to know quite a lot about fear. Hmmm," she considered Jones's comment. "Do you think he was saying you have to conquer your fear before it conquers you?"

"Makes sense. Any idea how I can pull that one off?"

"Maybe you can use your anger to block out the sportswriters and fans, to get so angry you don't care what they say about you."

"It won't take much effort to get a little angrier, that's for sure. In fact, it would be a pleasure."

Chapter 8

HOGAN GETS EVEN

AT THE END of his self-imposed deadline to win or quit, Ben arrived in the storybook village of Pinehurst, North Carolina. Nestled in the heart of the South, it was a romantic turn-of-the-century resort built around golf course architect Donald Ross's masterpiece, Pinehurst No. 2.

The entire village and golf course was owned by the Tufts family, that had become gracious hosts to the touring pros. Pros and their families received free room and board at what is now a five-star hotel, the Carolina, for one week. The Tufts deliberately created this unusually welcoming atmosphere to encourage gentlemanly competition, a return to the days of the true amateur who played for glory alone.

The aura of sportsmanship that filled the air in Pinehurst made the tournament more like an outing than a fight between the best golfers in the world. And because of the old-fashioned values engendered by the Tufts family, the North and South Open was treated as a major tournament. Its trophy, a bronzed putter boy, was revered among the pros.

If Ben had a chance of winning anywhere on tour, it was here where caustic sportswriters would find no ink for their pens.

Pinehurst No. 2 was also one of Ben's favorite golf courses. The love Donald Ross lavished on this, his favorite mistress, had created a hallowed experience in golf. Ross knew how to toy with the mind of a golfer, and he designed his courses to make players work for their scores. Lost in the hushed pines, golfers faced nothing but the challenge Ross set before them.

The night before the tournament found Ben and Valerie in the cozy dining room of the Carolina Hotel. Valerie knew something was different about Ben, but she couldn't put her finger on the change. Perhaps it was the serenity of the old village, or perhaps it was a deeper shift in his psyche.

She intended to discover the source of his newfound comfort so was delighted with Ben's suggestion of a walk through the village after dinner.

"I'm sorry, Val," he said softly, his voice punctuating the night air.

"For what, Ben?"

"For the pain we've had to go through in following my dream. For all those oranges. You know I still dream about oranges. Oranges, oranges, oranges. In some of my dreams, I even putt the damn things."

"We never really starved, Ben."

"I know, but I wanted to make things easier for you, like Byron did for Louise. My inability to win has kept me from taking care of you." Ben was thinking about the ranch Nelson was talking of buying.

"Ben, you've done a good job taking care of me. The other pros have their share of troubles, too. Their wives talk plenty between rounds. It seems everyone here has a set of problems to overcome."

"You mean everyone else is having problems, like us?"

"Yes. I've never told you about them. I didn't want to destroy your focus with gossip about the rest of the tour."

"There are some things I haven't told you, too. Two weeks ago, I almost decided to go home. But then I thought, 'If you quit now, you might miss out on the win right around the corner.'"

"Oh, Ben, please don't quit. I know you'll get past this barrier soon, and then there'll be no holding you back. Please, just a little while longer."

"I'll try."

The following day, Ben quickly found himself in a typical Hogan fight against par and the course. Secretly, as he teed his ball, he told himself, "It's now or never," and the decision to quit, to stop caring about his fans, the sportswriters, about failing, gave him a freedom he had not known.

After nine holes, Ben was three under par. He knew if he could do as well on the back nine, the field would have a tough time matching his six-under score.

Some people believe in predestination, some in luck. Ben believed in what he could make happen, and the second nine was a good example of his beliefs. Totally absorbed in golf, he thought about his score only once, when he was walking up the 18th fairway with the six-under he had previously only dreamed about.

"Congratulations, Ben," Demaret beamed as they watched the officials post their scores on the leader board.

"Thanks," Ben said without glancing in Demaret's direction. He was too engrossed in his game to notice who had spoken to him.

The second day of play was a repeat of the first. Ben was three under after the first nine, lost in the same smooth groove of straight shots and deadly putts.

Then, coming up the 18th fairway just as he was about to shoot a 66 for the day, an old nemesis joined Ben. His fear of failure returned and took over his game.

Ben's pushed five-iron approach drifted right and kicked off Donald Ross's slanted 18th green into a swale on the back right-hand side. It was one of Ross's mind tricks. Bogey.

Walking to the scorer's table, he glowered at the scorecard in his hand. A bogey on the 18th, when he should have had a par.

"How'd you do today, Ben?" Byron Nelson asked, interrupting Ben's mental conversation with Donald Ross about problems with slippery pine needles on the course.

"Bogeyed the damn 18th for a 67."

"Whew, I believe that's a new tour record for thirty-six holes, Ben. Nice going," Nelson said, patting Ben on the back.

"I hope that bogey doesn't come back to haunt me."

Ben walked back to the hotel and met Valerie in the foyer.

"Got the lead again, 133 at the halfway mark."

"How wonderful! Let's celebrate."

"I don't want to celebrate yet, Val. The tournament's not over."

Ben arrived at the practice area early the next morning. He didn't want another missed shot today, especially when he had the lead.

Despite the extra practice, Ben's third round was a disappointment. Putts weren't dropping, approaches didn't land where they were aimed, even his driving was off. Ben never got into the rhythm of his game. He worked as hard as he could, but finished the day with a 74.

Valerie met a scowl for dinner.

"I let them all back in," Ben reported. "I had such a great lead, and now I gave them all another shot at the trophy."

"Ben, just because you have one bad day doesn't mean the tournament is lost. Remember Oakland?"

Ben didn't say anything, but it was clear that he was listening and wanted Valerie to go on.

"Whatever it takes, Ben, you can do it tomorrow. Today is gone and yesterday doesn't matter anymore."

"Hmmm. I am in a good position."

"Whatever it takes, Ben. You can do it."

The next morning, on the practice green, Ben realized the difference between this tournament and the one in Oakland, when his tires were stolen.

"I didn't have time to get nervous," he thought to himself. "I was so damn mad about those tires, I jumped out of Snead's car and ran to the 1st hole and teed off."

Suddenly, all of the frustration Ben had been carrying around with him bubbled to the surface. "I've had it with this game. I'm gonna win today." In anger, Ben threw his clubs back into his bag and strode to the 1st tee.

There, he impatiently waited for his cue to start. He looked neither to the right nor the left, neither to the fans nor to the officials. He stared straight ahead at Donald Ross's pines, at the little red flag that held the magic balm for his anger.

After nine holes, Ben was three under par. Each tap into the cup, every sound of hard rubber grating on metal, stoked his anger. He barely stayed on a green long enough to see his putt drop before he marched to the next hole like a parade marshal, without waiting for his playing partner or caddy to catch him. It was obvious he was marching to a different drummer.

Trouble struck on the long par-five 10th hole, however. Ben was a little too aggressive and shot his first bogey. A par on the next hole told him that he had settled his anger back to the right level, and he continued at par all the way through 15.

On the 16th tee, his caddy told him he had a six-stroke lead, and that his closest competitors, Sam Snead and Byron Nelson, were folding. The information broke Ben's spell.

It was a struggle for Ben to par the 16th and 17th holes. He was out of his rhythm now, and all his efforts to steady himself failed.

Ben bogeyed the 18th hole again and walked to the scorer's table, leaving his caddy rushing behind him.

As Ben checked over his score before turning in his card, his out-of-breath caddy arrived with his bag.

"If you ever caddy for me again, don't tell me how someone else is doing," Ben snapped as he picked up his bag and walked off the course.

The embarrassed caddy shrugged and glanced at Ben's scorecard. He had scored a 70 that day and was five strokes ahead of Snead and Nelson, who were still out on the course.

In the clubhouse, Ben sought out a phone and called

Valerie. "If Snead or Nelson don't decide to pull off another miracle finish, we've got it," he said.

"I was just on my way out to the course." Valerie was out of breath from a hurried packing and, now, from Ben's exciting news. "You finished up early. What happened out there today?"

"I lost my concentration on the back nine again."

"Maybe it won't matter this time, Ben."

"If it does, I'm going home," Ben said, matter-of-factly.

Valerie didn't wait for the hotel's bus to take her to the course. She called the front desk for a ride and rushed to be with Ben. She found him pacing behind the scorer's table.

"If Snead doesn't burn it up on the way home, we're in." Ben threw his cigarette on the ground and lit another. Smoking had been a habit for several years, especially at the end of a tournament when his emotions were raw. It was as though the smoke gave him one more screen to hide behind. But it wasn't just cigarette nerves that made Ben worry about Snead's finish today. Snead had a reputation for going on a birdie binge when he saw a tournament he could snatch from a fellow player.

"How are we doing?" Valerie asked, still out of breath.

"Last I heard, Snead was on the 14th hole and four strokes behind. Byron's four strokes behind, but he's on the 16th."

"Let me be the first to congratulate you," Valerie said as she hugged Ben.

"I hope you're right. This road's been so damn long."

"This one is yours, Ben. You're so far out in front this time; they won't be able to catch you. You did what you needed to do to win." As Valerie looked at Ben's tightly drawn face, she saw a small tear in his eye that no amount of smoke could hide.

A sea of people jumped into sight, distracting them and giving Ben a chance to regain his composure. Looking past the 18th hole where Nelson was finishing, Ben realized the crowd was following Snead on the 16th.

Ben walked over the scorer's table and discovered Nelson was out of the hunt. Snead had parred both 14 and 15. That meant he would now have to eagle the par-five 16th and birdie 17 and 18 to tie.

"Of all the golfers on tour, why is it always Snead who still has a chance to take my first trophy away?" Ben asked.

"Not much longer now," Valerie said as she pushed her small frame up against Ben's to steady him. "You've worked hard for this for years. Today is the day."

Ben walked a short way down the 18th fairway so that he could hear the reaction of Snead's fans. He lit cigarette after cigarette as he tried to determine what was happening, Valerie rushing behind.

"Relax, Ben. There's nothing more to be done now. No matter what, you did your best."

"I should have birdied that 15th hole. I left the putt sitting like a hot potato on the edge. If it had dropped, we'd be celebrating now instead of being spectators."

Ben heard groans coming from the 17th green.

"The fans are trying to tell you something," Valerie said with a big smile on her face.

"Oh my God, I can't believe it," he said, realizing that he had, finally, won. "As soon as I get my hands on that Putter Boy trophy, I'm never gonna let go. You'll have to drive."

As Ben made his way into the locker room, the reporters swooped around the winner.

"Can we talk to you about your victory, Ben?"

Cleaning out his locker, Ben looked over his shoulder and said, "Shoot."

Bill Jones of the *New York Times* led off. "There's been a rumor going around that unless you won, you weren't going to stay on tour after the end of the year. True or false?"

"That's pretty accurate. I came out here to win. Since I hadn't been doing that, I could see no sense in continuing the process of playing runner-up, as you guys have so accurately and repeatedly reported."

"Well, now that you have won, are you going to set any new goals?"

"I would expect that my wife is already picking out some new goals for the both of us to shoot for," Ben said with unaccustomed laughter.

"Just how much does your wife figure into your success on tour?"

"As much as she can." Ben laughed again and realized he was enjoying a session with reporters for the fist time. "Seriously, fellows, if it wasn't for my wife, I wouldn't be on tour and I wouldn't have won today."

"What was the main thing you did today that you haven't done before, Ben?"

"Hook less. I've had as many problems with a hook creeping into my swing as the rest of the tour put together. Maybe now I'll be able to hit the fairways more often and give myself more good lies."

"Was there anything else that contributed to your victory here?"

Ben turned around and looked squarely into the eyes of a writer who just a few weeks before had categorized him as a tour hanger-on.

"Yes," he answered. "I shot a lower score than the rest of the field."

Ben's score of 277 did not just amount to a lower score. It set a new record for a tournament that was considered a major.

Two days later, at the Greensboro Open, he did it again. After shooting 69 to tie for the lead with Clayton Heafner, Ben shot rounds of 68, 66, and 67 to win by three strokes. The next day, he traveled to the Land of the Sky Open in Asheville and shot 67-68-69-69 to beat Ralph Guldahl by three strokes.

In the span of eleven days, Ben had played ten rounds in the 60s: 216 holes of tournament golf in thirty-four under par. He had charged up Hogan's hill with a vengeance, and only the shadow of a world war could hold him back again.

Chapter 9

THE SHADOW EMERGES

"Did you have anything to do with my stateside posting?" Ben asked Bobby Jones when he returned from military service in 1946.

"How wonderful to hear from you, Drill Sergeant Hogan."

"You didn't answer my question, Bob. Are you still in the intelligence service and keeping secrets?"

"Oh, no, Ben, I was discharged the same as the rest of you guys. To answer your question, it's one of those things I can't say yes or no to. Ed Dudley called me after he received a letter from President Roosevelt asking the PGA to schedule exhibition matches to boost the morale of the home folks. I told him he'd have to arrange stateside postings for the professionals in order to comply."

"I wondered how I got so lucky. I was able to keep up my practice routine and that meant a lot to me."

"Did you learn anything new?"

"Well, Val says I act like a drill sergeant on the practice range now, giving orders and expecting the balls to march up to the tee in formation."

Jones laughed hard, knowing Valerie had described Ben's perfect practice round. "Ben, if anyone can get those balls to behave, it's you."

In the spring of 1946, Ben returned to the pro tour and merely picked up where he left off by winning at Portland, Phoenix, St. Petersburg, and in Texas at the San Antonio Open and at the Miami Four-ball with his Texas friend and rival, Jimmy Demaret.

In years to come, winning five tournaments in three months would be an impossible task for golf pros. But in his first year back on tour after the war, Ben was just getting started on one of the great years in sports history.

Arriving at the 1946 Masters, Ben granted an interview to a sportswriter at Bobby Jones's request. Jones secretly hoped Ben would win the respect of the sportswriters and avoid the pain he suspected was headed Ben's way. But even the most powerful name in the game of golf could not hold back the tide of destiny.

"It's a beautiful day to be playing," the writer said to Ben as they walked under the old live oak tree near the clubhouse on their way to the practice area. His nickname was Tex, an indication of the state he called home. Jones had left nothing to chance.

"And a beautiful day to be writing," Ben smiled back, doing his share.

Ben arrived at his favorite practice spot, gave his caddy instructions, and spent fifteen minutes warming up.

"Do you always spend so much time loosening up?" Tex asked him.

"Only if I want to play well," Ben kidded back. "Besides,

while I'm loosening up, I also try to figure out how my body feels. All days are not the same. Temperature and humidity change things. Even the amount of rest you get dramatically affects the way your body performs." Ben wondered how much Tex knew about the game of golf.

"Every day is a new day, then?"

"For the most part," Ben said, hoping to give Tex what he wanted for a good story. "The important thing is to find out how my body will perform today." Ben then took out his eight-iron and hit a few shots.

"Let's take my eight-iron. I'll hit it out for a while to find out how my rhythm and timing are doing." Ben tried a few easy shots that looked slow and graceful to Tex.

"They look right on the money," Tex offered, as he watched Ben hit six shots just right of his caddy.

"Maybe to you, but these shots tell me I'm a little slow and lazy today and that I'd better play my shots more to the left." Ben hit a gentle fade to demonstrate.

"If all the dubs would learn to read their shots on the practice range and react to what they see, they would be able to hit the ball much better," Ben explained and then hit his first drive, and it rolled to a stop at his caddy's feet.

"Beautiful," Tex gushed. "Wouldn't it be great if we could get golfers all over the country to hit 'em like that."

"Well, thanks, Tex. Now for the lesson," Ben said as he lit another cigarette. "There are three things a ball tells you when you hit it."

Tex started writing.

"There's the trajectory, the direction of the shot, and, lastly, the way the ball finishes, tailing left, right, or straight."

Ben hit another ball. "See that shot? It tailed slightly right at the end, telling me the club face was open at impact."

Ben hit another that finished with a slight draw. "Now that shot told me the club face came into the ball slightly closed."

"Where did you learn all this?" Tex asked, mesmerized by Ben's knowledge of golf.

"On practice ranges all over the country."

"Can you hit any kind of shot you want to?"

"Well, let's test it out. Why don't you tell me what you want me to hit and I'll try my best to give you what you want," Ben said, hoping the sportswriter would pick out a challenging shot and not some god-awful thing that couldn't be played on a golf course.

"How about a high, long fade?"

Ben complied.

"Beautiful," Tex commented as he watched the shot. "How about a long, low draw?"

Ben smiled, knowing he had mastered that shot years ago.

"Beautiful," Tex said again.

For a writer, Ben thought, Tex had very few words in his vocabulary.

"Trajectory is accomplished by how you come into the ball," Ben continued. "A steep inclined swing will give you a high trajectory. A low flat swing will give you a long, low shot. Direction is accomplished by how you swing through the ball. And, finally, your final fade or draw is accomplished by how you angle the club head as you impact the ball." Ben finished his lesson with another shot that went straight out, climbed and finished with a small fade.

"What about straight shots?" Tex asked.

Ben drew his driver back and stroked an expert shot that stayed straight on line.

"Like that?" Ben smiled.

"Beautiful," Tex offered.

"Straight shots are fickle and hard to count on. You're better off working the ball either right or left because you can count on pulling the shot off," Ben said, hitting another shot that went straight and then drew slightly. "That was supposed to go straight all the way," he added, hoping Tex was beginning to catch on.

"So you never try to hit a straight ball?" Tex asked.

"Well, let's just say I don't try to hit as many as the amateur golfers do."

"Thanks a lot, Ben," Tex finished. "Now maybe some of your fans will be able to understand what to do out here on the range."

"If they just experiment and listen to what their shots tell them, they'll be able to apply it to their games and lower their scores," Ben added, hoping his last remarks would make it into newspaper copy.

"Thanks, Ben," Tex smiled.

The next morning, Ben ran into Jimmy Demaret at breakfast.

"Thought you were going to get off to a new start, partner," Demaret said as he flopped a newspaper onto the table.

"Yeah," Ben replied. "I gave an interview yesterday to a writer who was trying to develop a new storyline for the fans. The interview went really well."

"Well, here's his new storyline," Jimmy said. "It's a doozy."

The headline read, TEXAS ICEBERG LISTENS TO BALLS.

Ben was speechless. On his face was the steely, hard look he donned whenever he thought he had been conned.

Stomping back to his hotel room, Ben complained to Valerie. "You won't believe this," he said, pitching the newspaper onto the bed. "Look."

Valerie glanced at the story and looked back at Ben, shaking her head in wonder.

"I tried," Ben pleaded. "I was as nice to this guy as a person could be. I slowed down and escorted him through my thoughts. I gave him the secrets everyone's been hounding me for. Then, instead of delivering the tips to the fans, he makes a point of mocking me."

Valerie crossed her arms, as if she could defend herself and Ben against the world's injustice. On a deeper level, she was afraid. She worried that sportswriters interfered with Ben's game, and she wondered how many strokes this article would cost. "I'm sorry, Ben," she said.

Ben ran his hands through his hair, dismayed at the persistence of the sportswriters to portray him as an uncaring man. "I don't think there's any way to get them on my side, Val. I did everything Bob told me to do. It was a great interview." Framing his face with his hands, his elbows on his knees, Ben stared at the floor. He was looking for a way out of the maze.

When Ben spoke again, his voice betrayed a resolve that left no doubt about where he stood as a man. Looking up into Valerie's tearful eyes, he said, "If I have to make a choice between earning the respect of the reporters and winning, Val, I'll take winning."

If Ben had been able to read the future, he would have known exactly why he had been betrayed. Like the other news hounds in his pack, the sportswriter had sniffed a story. It wasn't visible to the naked eye yet, but it was there and the writers were betting their careers on it. Ben was different from other golfers. He had a secret. When he revealed it, they knew it would be a big story, maybe the biggest in sports history, and each of them wanted to be the first to get it. Because of this, they were never going to let him out of their grasp.

As Ben played in the following weeks, his mind was on the PGA Championship, the last big event for the year. Winning a major championship was the next plateau of Hogan's hill.

The PGA Championship that year was being played at the Portland Golf Course, and in 1946 it had not switched to medal play like the other tournaments. The PGA was still match play.

Ben and Valerie arrived early so Ben could practice, and their strategy paid off. Ben won his first four matches and was about to start his fifth and final match, against Porky Oliver, when the enormity of winning a major tournament struck his nerves.

"I hope I can get into my game fast, like I did yesterday," Ben said to Valerie at breakfast after an early morning practice session. "I don't want to throw away any opportunities today." Ben took a sip of juice. He would rather have had a cup of coffee, but coffee jangled his nerves, and they were already too raw.

"Porky is no slouch in match play," Ben added. Oliver had beaten four famous players in the tournament, while

Ben's only well-known victim was Jimmy Demaret.

Valerie looked across the table at Ben. "Neither are you, Ben Hogan. You're getting better and better. Everyone out here knows it." She leaned closer to Ben, as though she could argue him into believing in himself. "You beat Frank Moore and Jimmy Demaret. They're no slouches either."

Ben looked at her. "Now, Val, you know as well as I do that Porky went up against a better pack of guys than I did. He had to get past Dick Metz, Chandler Harper, Byron, and finally, Jug McSpaden to get into the final round."

"And you shot 137 in qualifying while Porky trailed in with 147 and almost missed the cut."

Ben smiled. "You're right. What was the cutoff? 148?"

"Yep," Valerie grinned, knowing she had made her point. She loved winning arguments with Ben when they concerned his talent.

The first eighteen holes went quickly as Ben and Porky Oliver alternated hot runs. But Oliver's runs lasted longer than Ben's, and at the lunch break, Ben found himself three holes down.

"He's on and I'm struggling," Ben sighed to Valerie.

"You're only halfway through. You can turn this around."

Ben smiled at her. "Sometimes, I wish I had you inside my head when I'm out there."

"With all that golf stuff in there," Valerie said as she knocked the side of her head for emphasis, "your head would pop."

Ben laughed and then thought out loud, "I set the tour record on this course last year, didn't I?" The year before,

Ben had won the Portland Invitational by nine strokes while shooting a tour record of 261. It was an unbelievable twenty-seven strokes under par, which made a powerful statement that he was back from the army.

"You deserve this trophy as much as anyone, with all the practicing you do."

Ben grew more excited as he ate his lunch. "God, I was on my game here last year. It was as if all those years in the service when I couldn't play in a tournament came out of me in four great rounds."

"It will be a long time before your twenty-seven under is beaten, Ben."

Ben folded his hands under his chin, thinking. "If I remember correctly, my last two rounds were 63 and 64." Ben's eyes stared straight ahead as he watched the rounds play through in his head. "Those rounds would beat anyone today."

Ben threw his napkin onto his plate and leaned over to kiss Valerie as he got up. "Thanks."

"My pleasure, Mr. Hogan," she said.

Ben returned to the practice tee to warm up. His steps were the same ones he had used to march his recruits around the base. Chomping on his cigarette, he sent shot after shot toward its target.

"You got a minute?" a sportswriter said to Ben as he headed for the tee.

"Not now, Herb," Ben shot back without breaking his stride.

"This will only take a minute, Ben, and I have a pressing deadline," the sportswriter remarked, running beside Ben to catch up.

"I doubt your deadline is more pressing than mine. Are you three holes down?"

The sportswriter stopped, shook his head, and watched Ben march into the distance toward the tee.

Ben climbed onto the tee and faced the hole. He still had a few minutes before his tee time. As he sucked on his last cigarette before play, he stared at the point where he wanted his first shot to land. Then, he saw himself hitting his second shot and crossed his arms as he watched himself putt in the distance. Birdie. He butted the cigarette and continued staring at the hole as his caddy arrived.

"Ladies and gentlemen," the starter announced, "Mr. Porky Oliver from Wilmington, Delaware, leads Mr. Ben Hogan from Fort Worth, Texas, by the score of three holes. Mr. Oliver has the honor on the tee. Play away."

Ben's concentration did not break. He continued to stare at the hole. He was standing on the tee in one of the biggest golf championships in the world, on a course where he held the record for the best four rounds and the best single round. He owned the course and he knew it. His last thoughts were, "And I'll be damned if anyone's going to take it away from me."

Ben walked over to his bag and grabbed his driver before his caddy could pull it out and hand it to him. He felt his anger building. He was upset with himself for not having the honor on a course he had played better than anyone else in golf.

As Oliver teed off, Ben never saw the shot. He was in his own world and everything else was out of focus.

As Ben hit his drive, it was as if every bad piece of luck that had come his way could be wiped out with one stroke.

His ball flew past Oliver's and gave him a three-club advantage on his approach shot into the narrow green.

Hole after hole, Ben played as if each shot was the deciding factor of his life. Every drive, every approach, every putt was crucial to him. Slowly, relentlessly, it became obvious to everyone watching the PGA tournament that Ben Hogan could not be beaten.

Ben won six out of the first nine holes to go from three down to three up. He continued to burn up the course on the back nine. There was no letup in Ben. The memory of all his past struggles were wiped out with this one great round. No one had ever seen the kind of game Ben was capable of playing when he was angry, but they did that day.

Ben beat Oliver six and four. It was the worst thrashing in the finals of match play since Paul Runyan had beaten Sam Snead eight years before. By refusing to allow himself to shoot no worse than par, Ben had birdied eight of the fourteen holes they played, and if the match had gone on for a full eighteen holes he would have set another course record.

Winning the PGA fueled Ben's enthusiasm, and he won his next event, the Golden State Open, without challenge. He went on to win the Dallas Open, a Texas event that meant more to him than any other tournament except the PGA. Ben repeated his Texas win with another one at the North and South Open in Pinehurst.

Ben won thirteen tournaments in 1946, including two four-ball events with Jimmy Demaret. His winnings totaled $42,500, catapulting him into first place in the money standings. The Vardon Trophy for the lowest scoring average wasn't awarded that year because of the war, but had one been given, he would have taken that too.

Ben's incredible year was the chief conversation among sportswriters, as speculation about his abilities mounted.

"What do you think of Hogan, Cal?" one sportswriter asked another as they headed toward the locker room searching for interviews. "Think he'll be able to keep it up?"

"Nah. Inside," he said, thumping his breast, "where it counts, Hogan's no champion. He'll fold. You can bet on it."

Although Ben never heard their private comments, he knew what the sportswriters were saying about him. He knew they believed his victories in '46 to be an aberration, something he would never be able to repeat. Locked in a struggle only fate would interrupt, Ben and the sportswriters pushed and pulled at each other for history's top honors.

Ben started out the new tour year of 1947 by winning the Los Angeles Open, his first win there since 1942. Although he played well in his next two events, he lost, but he won again in Phoenix. He lost the Masters, however, and the dance was on.

As Ben and Valerie were leaving Augusta for the next stop on tour, the new Colonial Invitational in Texas, Ben raised a subject that would have a dramatic impact on his game.

"Val, some of the guys have recommended that I write a book." Ben squirmed slightly in his seat, something he did only when he was wrestling with a dilemma.

"A book?" Valerie said, astonished. She knew Ben disliked publicity.

"Yes, they're convinced I've got secrets I'm not sharing. I guess they think a book about technique will lay it all out for them, and they'll be able to figure out what I'm hiding."

Valerie laughed. "I thought you told them the truth, that you just apply what you learn in practice."

"I've told 'em, Val, and I've told 'em and told 'em again. They don't believe me." Ben banged the steering wheel, then sighed as though the subject exhausted him.

"So how do you think a book will help? It's just not like you to go after the limelight, Ben."

"Well, I've got another idea in mind. I figure a book might just get the reporters off my back."

"Get the reporters off your back?" Valerie was shocked. "How on earth do you think a book is going to do that?"

"Here's the way I've got it figured. If I go straight to the fans with the things I've learned, it'll help them take strokes off their scores. Then, maybe the word will get out that I'm a nice guy. After that, maybe, just maybe, the reporters will give me a fair chance.

"How can I lose? At the very worst, everyone will stop bugging me about keeping secrets." Ben was quiet, giving Valerie time to formulate her answer, but his impatience quickly broke through.

"What do you think? Do you think it's a good idea?"

"I think you've got something here. I don't know what will happen, but I think it's worth a try."

Ben was silent, not excited as she expected him to be after winning her approval. She knew he was keeping something from her.

"You'd better tell me the whole story, Ben."

Ben laughed. "Val, sometimes I think you can read my

mind! Okay, I'll level with you. Do you remember what happened to Ralph Guldahl?" Ben stole a glance at Valerie as she shook her head.

"Well, Ralph was so good so fast, he left for California as soon as he turned pro and then won the Western Open, the Masters, and the U.S. Open. Someone convinced Ralph that what he had done was worth writing about, so he spent a couple of the war years dissecting his game." Ben glanced at Valerie, who was intently listening to his story.

"He never hit another good shot in a tournament. The reporters say he wouldn't even be a decent caddy now." Ben sighed and shook his head.

"So what are you trying to tell me?"

"Some of the guys think it was because of the book. They think he overanalyzed his game, broke it into little pieces to show how each stroke is played, and then he couldn't put his game back together again."

"Oh, Ben," Valerie laughed. "You worry about the strangest things."

"It's not strange, Val. What if that happened to me? Golf is all I've got. I'd rather die than have to give up golf."

Seeing that Ben was indeed worried about Guldahl's legacy, Val stopped laughing and took his concerns seriously.

"Ben, no one can take your game away from you. No one except you. If writing a book is part of your game, then play it your way, and don't look back."

Word about Ben's book spread and he found himself favored to win an important tournament for the first time. It was the tournament the pros called the "big one," the U.S. Open, to be played in 1947 at the St. Louis Country Club.

"Do you enjoy being favored?" a sportswriter from *St. Louis Dispatch* asked Ben as he arrived for practice several days before tournament play was scheduled to begin.

"Sure. It's an honor, but it won't mean anything unless I can match it with a win," Ben replied honestly.

Believing he had found Ben in an unusually talkative mood, the sportswriter pressed on. "What do you think about the new challenge from Bobby Locke? Do you think he should be playing over here in our Open?" Bobby Locke was the new rising star in golf and he was a South African. Jealousy toward Locke was growing among the American pros, and the sportswriter was hoping to involve Ben in the controversy.

"It's called an Open," Ben replied, choosing his words carefully, "because it's supposed to be open to all golfers." This was an unprecedented chance for Ben to get his views, his real personality, into print – and he knew it. "If you want to prove yourself," he continued, "you want to do it in these national events that bring out all the best golfers from everywhere. Most of our original Opens were won by golfers who were born outside our shores. After all, the game of golf is not originally an American game."

The sportswriter wrote down every word, and Ben's hopes for an accurate portrayal soared. "I understand you're working on your first golf book," he asked. "Will it explain how you've managed to be so successful since the end of the war?"

"It will if you realize any success in golf has to do with practice."

"Will it tell us your secrets?"

Ben tensed, visibly annoyed at the suggestion he was

hiding something. "Anyone can find the same secrets I've found by practicing as much as I have," Ben replied.

"Then you do have secrets?" the sportswriter asked.

"To my knowledge," Ben explained, "there is nothing I do that hasn't been done by someone before. So in all honesty, I can't label them as secrets."

"Then why are you writing the book?"

"Well, to contribute to the growth and knowledge of the game and to help all the regular dubs play better." Ben shuffled his feet, growing uneasy at the sportswriter's relentless questions.

"And to make a few bucks?" the sportswriter asked.

Ben glared at the sportswriter, then slowly picked up his bags to leave. "Anything you do and do well in our society, including sportswriting, makes money. I play golf to win by doing something I love. Money is a by-product. I'm writing a book to help other golfers understand the game better. That's all there is to it."

The next morning on the practice tee, Toney Penna, a fellow MacGregor rep, greeted Ben.

"Hey Ben, this morning's paper said you were writing a golf book."

"Yep, that's right, Toney," Ben said as he drew his six-iron out of his bag.

"The article said you weren't going to tell us any of your secrets," Toney smiled. "You wouldn't be holding out on an old friend, would you?"

"That's what they printed?" Ben said loudly, clearly agitated. "All these reporters ever want to do is stoke up controversy. I'm sick of it." Penna nodded but remained silent, knowing this wasn't a topic he wanted to pursue.

Ben didn't win the U.S. Open, and although he won seven tournaments in 1947, none of them were majors. The gains he had made in 1946 seemed to be slipping. After failing to defend his PGA Championship title, he turned to his best friend for support.

"Well, Val," Ben said as they traveled home to Fort Worth, "I think that book did more harm than good."

"How can you say that after all your hard work? Rushing to Augusta National between tournaments to record practice sessions for the book, then coming home to look over the drawings and write the script. Why, even Bob Jones says it's an extraordinary book, that it will become a bible to golfers all over the world.

"You're not thinking your game is falling apart like Guldahl's, are you?" Valerie was concerned.

"No, Val," Ben said, laughing and easing the tension. "But something's wrong. No majors and down from thirteen to seven wins. That doesn't spell progress to me."

Valerie wanted to tell her husband he was being too hard on himself, but she knew to trust Ben's intuition. If he said something was wrong, then it was. She was quiet for a long time.

"Ben," Valerie began. "I think I know what it is."

Ben turned to look at her.

"I think it's all the activity."

Ben paused, clearly puzzled. "What activity?"

"Well, let's add it all up. There's the Bobby Locke situation. The guys are always trying to drag you into it, and you always decline, but it must bother you. Then, there's the Ryder Cup. You're up for captain for the first time. And that golf grip venture Jack Burke wants you to get in on. That uses up a little more of your concentration. On top of all this, there's the book. In fact, I'm surprised you have any time for golf at all!"

Ben sat back, seeing Valerie's point. "When you put it that way, Val, I see what you mean."

Valerie looked out the window at the passing scenery, waiting for Ben to take it all in and realize what he had to do.

"What would I ever do without you?" Ben finally replied.

Tears came to Valerie's eyes. She was touched by his words, but most of all she was glad she had guessed the source of the problem. "Without me, you'd probably load yourself up with a few more distractions that would take you further away from your game," she said.

Ben decided to play a limited schedule in 1948, concentrating his time on just the tournaments he really liked. As he did so, he put into motion a series of events that made the sportswriters' hunches about a secret come true.

The first tournament of the new year, the Los Angeles Open, was played at one of Ben's favorite courses, the Riviera Country Club. Ben's newfound focus was noticed by the sportswriters, who now referred to him as the "Mechanical Man," and by his fellow players, who started calling him "The Hawk" because of the keen, piercing look in his eyes.

Ben rather liked being called The Hawk; it was certainly more flattering than being identified as inhuman and mechanical. However, he ignored them all and concentrated on making small refinements to his swing that enabled him to approach his target from either side and from any height.

Consequently, Ben won the Los Angeles Open by setting a new record of 275, five strokes under the old tournament record. The course was nicknamed "Hogan's Alley," and Ben's fellow pros talked about conceding the U.S. Open to him that year because it was going to be played at Riviera.

But Ben wasn't worried about the U.S. Open yet. He wanted to win the Masters. In 1948, the Masters was not considered a major tournament. However, it was Bobby Jones's tournament.

The Masters that year did not go to Ben. It belonged to Claude Harmon, a club professional from Winged Foot who led from the second round to beat Cary Middlecoff by five strokes. Ben didn't even get to play his traditional pre-tournament round with Bobby Jones. Ill health was beginning to plague Jones, preventing him from keeping up with social commitments the way he had in past years.

With the wind ruffling their hair and the sound of highway miles separating them from their lost Masters, Ben and Valerie drove to St. Louis and the PGA Championship.

Ben qualified at 138 for thirty-six holes, which put him fifth behind Stewart Alexander at 134, as well as Toney Penna, Sam Snead, and Jimmy Demaret. Ben knew it would take an enormous effort to win. Golf had sustained a postwar boom, and huge crowds turned out to see the pros play. In response, the players had all finely tuned their games, and they were now a tough group to beat.

In his first round, Ben and his opponent, Jock Hutchinson, Jr., finished tied for eighteen holes. Ben had fired one of his best rounds of the year, but it was not good enough to win. In overtime holes, Ben and Hutchinson kept the pressure on each other, and it was only on the 23rd hole that Ben shot an unanswered birdie.

The second round found Ben needing a birdie on the 18th to avoid another playoff. This time, he got it and won one up over Johnny Palmer.

Grueling thirty-six-hole matches were next. Ben met Gene Sarazen who had easily won his first matches. After the first eighteen holes, Ben stood four up, and it looked as though he was in command of the match. Sarazen fought back and was one down with one hole to go as they faced the 18th. Ben parred this last hole and stood nervously by as Sarazen attempted a twelve-foot birdie putt. He missed, and Ben won, one up.

In his next match against Chick Harbert, Ben led by five after the morning eighteen holes. But he then put his game on the back burner, and Harbert took advantage of the slip, coming back to two down with two to go. The Hawk refired his game and closed out the match on the 17th, winning three and one.

Ben now faced his longtime Texas friend and rival, Jimmy Demaret. Both played brilliant golf and found their match tied after thirty-three holes as they each stood ten under par.

The end came into view on the 34th hole, as Demaret three-putted to lose the hole. Ben quickly closed out the match with a birdie on the 35th to win two and one.

The PGA Championship was almost Ben's. He had one

more thirty-six-hole match to play against Mike Turnesa, from the well-known golfing family in upstate New York.

Ben shot a morning round of 66 and took a four-up lead.

"Congratulations," a sportswriter said to Ben as he passed his lunch table. Ben barely heard it.

The afternoon round was much tighter as both players matched pars and birdies. Finally, both men fell under the spell of The Hawk, and Ben birdied the 28th, 29th, and 30th holes to win his second PGA Championship.

After a brief rest at home in Texas, Ben and Valerie drove to Los Angeles for the U.S. Open and Hogan's Alley.

The first round told Ben it was his tournament, as he birdied four of the first five holes to tie Lew Worsham for the lead at five under. Then, he slipped, a victim of too much confidence, and shot a 72 to fall one stroke behind Sam Snead.

On Open Saturday, Ben took his time and focused carefully on each shot. A hard-fought morning round of 68 put him in the lead – two strokes ahead of Jimmy Demaret and three ahead of Jim Turnesa.

Ben teed off in the afternoon to play another grueling eighteen holes. His play was stunning, without a hint of fatigue, until he came to the par-four 15th hole. Until then, his day had consisted of pars and birdies with the exception of one bogey in the morning round on this same hole.

Standing on the 15th tee, Ben picked up snatches of course gossip. Jimmy Demaret had finished with a new Open record score of 278. Demaret had become the first player to break the magical barrier of 280 in a U.S. Open championship, and Ben was distracted by the news.

Slowing down his play, Ben played the 15th too cautiously, taking another bogey. But the missed hole propelled him back into his anger and made him reset his concentration. It worked, and he finished by shooting a 69, two strokes in front of Demaret. His total of 276 set a new U.S Open record by five shots. He was the first Open champion to shoot three rounds in the 60s.

Winning two major championships in one year caused Ben to reach for the moon: He went on to finish his year with seven more wins, including another Western Open. He won a total of ten of the twenty-five tournaments he had entered in 1948 and was awarded the first Player of the Year trophy.

The start of 1949 matched Ben's dreams. He won two of his first four events and would have won a third if Jimmy Demaret had not forced, and won, a playoff. Keeping his promise to play a limited schedule, Ben headed home after the Phoenix Open.

When he was 640 miles from Fort Worth, Ben met his fate.

The day began like any other. Ben strolled out of his motel room for a breath of air and his traditional morning cigarette. As soon as he got outside, he realized the remaining miles would be difficult because of the fog that had rolled in from Mexico. The air was filled with thick, splotchy patches, allowing visibility of only six to ten feet.

Ben briefly thought about delaying the trip but decided

to go on for Valerie's sake. Valerie had been plagued with motion sickness all her life. Fog would help block the movement of the car and make the trip more comfortable for her.

Taking Highway 80 east, Ben was first able to take the car up to forty miles an hour, only to have to slow down to almost nothing because of the fog rolling in over the highway.

"Are you happy, dear?" Valerie said to him as they turned onto the mountain highway. "This morning's paper said you're the leading money winner on tour with close to $10,000 after only four events."

Hunched over the steering wheel to get a better view of the road, Ben said, "Money's a bad way of comparing results, Val. Next year, the tournaments will increase the purses. Pros will be able to play worse but still win more."

"I still wish they'd offered this kind of money when we first started on tour," she said wistfully. "We would have had an easier time of it."

After thinking quietly for a moment, Ben spoke. "In some ways, I'm glad they didn't. If they had, I might not have been so motivated. Survival is a big motivator, you know."

Ben moved even closer to the windshield. The road they were on had descended into a valley, and fog now enveloped the car. Ben couldn't see past the nose of the Cadillac, and he leaned forward in his seat while drastically slowing his speed.

Sensing Ben's mounting worry, Valerie sat up straight. It was the last movement she would make in the first new car they had ever owned.

"Val!"

Ben's scream came just as he threw himself over his wife. He saw two large headlamps coming directly for him, totally blocking the road and leaving no place to hide.

A Greyhound bus, trying to pass a tractor trailer in the fog, had collided with the Hogans and pushed their car backward along the road 250 feet before coming to a stop. Ben and Valerie slumped unconscious inside their demolished car.

Valerie was the first to awaken. Her head throbbed and she realized she couldn't move. Ben was pinned between her and the dashboard – and he wasn't moving.

Her head was pounding, and then she realized that it wasn't in her head, it was someone pounding on the car door. She looked and saw a face through her window.

The man pulled on the door but it wouldn't open. She tried to squirm in her seat to reach the door lock, but even that slight movement seemed to take so long.

The man yelled at her through the window to hurry. He seemed to be worried about the car catching fire. Valerie looked at Ben, but he didn't move.

She tried again to get to the lock. Her movements were slow and uncoordinated. Finally, she was able to pull up the lock, and it made a popping sound that echoed through the car.

The door opened and she fell backwards as someone's arms caught her and held her up. With strange arms under her, she was slowly dragged out of the car. She weakly called out to Ben.

Valerie was laid beside a culvert on the edge of the road, and she watched, dazed, as the man – was there only one or were there two? – went back for Ben. It seemed to take such a long time.

Valerie awoke abruptly. I must have drifted off, she

thought. A small group of people were kneeling on the ground over Ben.

"Cover him," one of them said with finality.

"No!" Valerie cried, and she used every bit of strength to go kneel beside Ben.

"He's done for, lady," the man said in an oddly factual tone. "We couldn't get no pulse."

Valerie pulled Ben's head onto her lap. "Ben, oh, Ben," she sobbed, holding onto his hand. She rocked him back and forth, sobbing and crying.

Somewhere in Ben, a tiny heartbeat responded to Valerie's pain. They had started on this road together, and together they would finish it.

Soon, the ambulance arrived and two men in white coats rushed out of its back doors.

"What's the situation here?" one of the medics asked.

One of the men who had stopped to pull Ben and Valerie out of the car answered. "The lady's okay, I think, but the guy's dead."

"He's not dead!" Valerie cried.

The medics crouched over Ben, checking his wrist for a pulse. "There's a pulse!" he shouted to the other ambulance driver. "It's weak, but it's there. Quick, let's get him out of here."

As Valerie climbed into the back of the ambulance, she saw Ben's golf clubs laying scattered on the ground behind the car, their iron shafts strangely gleaming against the black asphalt. As if to underscore the hope that so long as Ben was alive, he would one day need his clubs, someone moved to pick them up. That made Valerie feel better.

The next morning, newspapers carried their first front-page headline about Ben: GREYHOUND BUS ENDS MOST SPECTACULAR GOLF CAREER IN AMERICA: BEN HOGAN NEAR DEATH.

Chapter 10

HOGAN BECOMES THE FIRST COMEBACK KID

A NURSE AT BEN'S HOSPITAL called Valerie to the phone for an important call. She picked it up in the hallway, out of Ben's earshot, and when she heard the voice, she was glad she was alone.

"I'm sorry I'm calling so late, Val."

"Oh, Bob," Valerie sobbed, free at last to share her fear with the one person who would truly understand, Bobby Jones. "Ben's legs are crushed. He has eleven broken bones, and he's already been through surgery twice."

Valerie remembered how they had arrived at the Hotel Dieu Hospital in El Paso. The initial frenetic activity had been quickly replaced with silence and waiting.

Flowers arrived for Ben, and Valerie had no idea what to do with them. She still moved slowly, as if in a dream. Everything was difficult and filled with worry. The evening blended into day as she was told, "Ben's in the operating room. Ben's asleep. We hope he'll make it."

The nurses' comments haunted her. "Mrs. Hogan, what do you want us to do with the flowers?" The ever-present flowers.

Then, the telegrams arrived. Hundreds of them from all over the country. Hope you get well. We're praying for you. Newsmen and sportswriters arrived, but Valerie had nothing to tell them. There was one operation, then another. Ben was either in surgery, recuperating from surgery, sleeping, or resting up for another surgery.

Valerie waited. And worried. Ben might live. He might walk again, but golf? Out of the question. Now, hearing Bobby Jones's steady voice, the worry began to bleed out of her.

"So the news reports are correct," Jones said with a sigh of resignation.

"Yes, for once, they're correct." Valerie hurriedly brushed the tears from her eyes. "But what about your own news reports? Are you all right, Bob?" Although Jones had tried to keep the news from the public, reports had leaked about his recent hospital visit and had reached Valerie's ears.

"I'll be okay, Val. Don't worry about me. Worry about Ben." Jones had recently been diagnosed with syringomyelia, a slow, crippling neurological disease. It was, he thought, the darkest of nights for champions.

Putting his own worries aside, Jones began again, "How are you holding up, Val? This must all be terribly hard on you."

"I walked away from the accident with only a few bumps and bruises. Ben threw himself over me to protect me and almost killed himself in the process."

"What do the doctors say?"

"They think he'll live, but they don't know if he'll ever walk again. Bob, I just can't tell Ben the truth. He had me prop up his golf clubs in the corner of his room," Valerie said softly. "How can I tell him he may never play golf again? That he'll be lucky just to walk." Valerie's face was red and streaked with tears. Seeing her distress, one of the nurses brought her a box of tissues and quickly patted her on the back before giving her privacy once more.

"You must remember that doctors are not always right. They can't explain why one person survives an accident and why another does not, even if they sustain the same injuries. You know, Val, Ben's been through tough times before."

"But nothing like this, Bob, nothing like this."

"He'll make it. I know he will. This is just another test of his greatness. You'll see," Jones said with more hope than he felt.

"Please pray for us," Valerie added.

"Everyone in the country is praying for you. Tell Ben. It will help him," he said.

At first, there were no visitors. Ben Hogan was a private man, with no one in his inner circle save his wife. Even Valerie expected no more than perfunctory phone calls.

But the flowers kept arriving and with them, the mail.

Next came the sportswriters. Red Smith and Grantland Rice were only two of the many reporters who trickled into the hospital to write stories on Ben's condition. If Ben was feeling strong enough, he gave an interview. Almost to the man, each sportswriter left Ben's room with tears in his eyes. Most thought Ben lucky to be alive, and all thought he would never play golf again.

Valerie had to tell the nursing staff what to do with all the flowers and the mail. She was shocked to learn that hundreds of letters were being held, and hundreds more were arriving daily.

Slowly, Ben's condition improved. He had suffered a broken collarbone, a fractured pelvis, broken ribs, a broken ankle, and massive contusions to his legs, as well as a deep gash over his left eye. His left shoulder and left knee would need more surgery in the future, but for now, it was considered best that he rest and stabilize.

Valerie started a little ritual of reading some of the cards and letters to Ben in the evenings. He drifted so much between pain and medication that she wasn't sure he even knew she was there.

After two weeks, the doctors agreed to transfer Ben to Fort Worth. They didn't know if he would walk again, but they felt sure he would recover, given Valerie's ever-present nursing.

Then it struck.

Ben suffered a pulmonary embolism. A blood clot moved from one of his legs into his lung. If it had clogged a cardiac artery, it probably would have killed him.

Ben's trip home was canceled. If another clot moved, this time, he would surely die. The doctors held a meeting to discuss their options and decided that Ben's best chance was with a new form of surgery. A specialist was flown in and, again, Valerie waited while Ben struggled through yet another surgery.

As Valerie waited, she went through more cards and letters. The pile was amazing, and it was still growing. The fans' love for Ben warmed her. She never knew he had been so respected; she thought she'd been the only one to see the tender man who lurked behind the steely mask.

Ben's operation was successful. The doctors pronounced that he would live and even walk. That was enough for Ben – if he could walk, then he could play golf. He approached his recovery in the same way he approached a major tournament: He refused to give up.

Starting very slowly, still in bed and in pain, Ben decided to accomplish something toward his recovery every hour. Initially, he was only able to stretch his hands, opening and closing them again and again. Then, he graduated to squeezing little rubber balls. Soon, he dangled his legs over the side of the bed. Although these bedridden exercises were small, Ben knew he was focusing on the areas that enabled him to play golf. First the hands, then the arms, and then the body and legs.

The golf clubs Valerie had propped in the corner of his room were doing their job, and after a two-month hospital stay, Ben went home.

At first, he had to be content with merely stretching his legs, but then he began to hobble around the bedroom, and finally, he was able to walk around the house. Each day, he tried to walk farther and farther, pushing himself to relearn simple tasks as he had once pushed himself on the driving range.

Ben's recovery received an unexpected boost when he found Valerie sorting boxes of mail in their living room one morning about four months after the accident.

"Who are all these cards and letters from, Val?" he asked.

"Your fans."

"All of them?" A quick look told Ben there were hundreds, maybe thousands, of letters in front of Valerie.

"Isn't it wonderful? I thought they would stop now that you're home from the hospital, but they keep coming."

Ben was speechless for a moment. "You mean all these people took the time to write to me?" Ben stood over the mail, wanting to reach down and pick up one of the letters, but he was too shocked to move.

"Would you like to read one of them?" Valerie asked. "I read some of them to you in the hospital, but you were probably too groggy to pay attention."

"I remember the letters in the hospital, Val, but I thought you were making them up. You know, to cheer me up."

Valerie looked at Ben in surprise. "Of course they're real." In a joking voice she added, "And it'll take me a year to answer all of them. Here." She handed him a stack of mail. "Why don't you read a few?"

The first letter Ben read was from a couple in Minnesota.

Dear Ben,

We've watched you play in the Masters Tournament for years and have especially enjoyed what you do on the back nine. We live for the excitement of the last five holes every year in the Masters and cheer for you, always hoping you'll be the winner.

This year's Masters won't be the same without you. We pray that you'll get well and finally win at Augusta.

With much love,
Ralph and Hazel Mitti

Ben read another letter, and then another. By the time he finished his stack of mail, he had tears in his eyes. "You mean all these years, people were noticing me? They really cared what happened to me?" He was shocked.

"Oh, Ben," Valerie said, rushing to his side and guiding him into the wingback chair next to the fireplace.

"But, Val," Ben whispered as he squirmed in his chair, "I paid so little attention to them. I had to blank them out, so that they wouldn't interfere with my shots."

"Well, it looks as though they either didn't mind, or else they forgave you for it. Look around you at all this mail – you have thousands of fans."

Ben looked at her in disbelief. Still clutching a handful of letters, he read a few more. When he looked up, more tears glistened in the corners of his eyes.

"If I ever get to play golf again, I'm going to play for them."

Ben's recovery picked up speed after his discovery of the letters. No one except Valerie had seen the tears in his eyes as he walked laps around his bedroom or forced himself to hike up and down the hallway stairs. But three months after the accident, and only one month after his discharge from the hospital, he was chipping balls in his backyard.

Ben understood that his healing process was going to

be slow, but as the days passed and the progress was more visible to him, he became enthused about the future and his hopes for his golf career grew.

He practiced his swing every day as therapy for his body and mind. Just as he did when he had practiced with a golf ball, he didn't take a swing until everything was set. A swing was too important an effort to waste by not doing it right, regardless of the situation.

It took him weeks to get Valerie's approval to play a full round, but he finally wheedled it out of her. He felt belittled, having to use a golf cart in order to play the game he loved, but he tolerated it as a necessary price for being on the course again.

"I had a birdie on the 5th hole," Ben beamed to Valerie after coming home one afternoon, worn out from fighting the pain and being so out of shape.

"What was your total score?" Valerie asked, afraid of the question but knowing Ben expected her to ask it.

"76," Ben answered shyly.

"76?! Really a 76? That's wonderful, Ben, wonderful."

"But it's not tournament quality," he admitted. "I can do better, I promise you."

In early December, eleven months after his accident, Ben felt the old longing building within him. The entry date for the Los Angeles Open was fast approaching, and he thought about that date every day. Riviera was one of his favorite courses, and he wanted to play. But only if he could compete.

Encouraged by his fellow pros, Ben finally wrote the tournament committee and asked them to keep his entry a secret. He didn't want to let his newfound fans down if he had to pull out at the last minute. He still could not predict how his legs would feel from one day to the next.

Christmas came to Forth Worth, and Ben had not yet told Valerie about his decision to play. He knew she would not like the news, so he waited until the day after Christmas to tell her.

"I really think I ought to play," he said as gently as he could.

"It's only been eleven months since the accident, Ben." Valerie was uncharacteristically sharp.

She was worried about her husband. The doctors had warned her about the possibility of dangerous blood clots forming in Ben's legs from too much activity. One of them could still travel to his lungs or his heart and kill him.

Playing golf was one thing, competitive golf was quite another. And, she knew that with the added burden of physical pain, Ben might not be able to mentally play the game he once had. He had conquered his shyness by blocking out the crowds and ignoring the sportswriters. Could he do that as well as conquering the physical challenges?

No, Valerie thought, the risk was too great. Ben was hardest on himself. If he failed in front of so many people, it wouldn't matter that he had recovered from the accident. The rejection alone would kill him.

"I don't think it's a good idea," she said.

"C'mon Val," Ben countered.

She had never seen him so optimistic.

"Why not wait until you're fully recovered?" More than anything else, Valerie wanted to make sure her husband stayed alive.

"If I wait until I'm fully recovered, we might be waiting

forever."

"You've still got a limp," Valerie said, looking at his left leg.

"It's always going to be there," Ben said, rubbing his leg. "I'll take my time when I play."

Valerie cupped her chin in her hands and looked defeated.

"Look, Val," Ben said, his mind made up. "I'll never be able to play golf at the level I was used to. I accept that." Ben caught his breath. "I just want to compete."

Ben was Ben, she realized. Stubborn, determined, and in love with the game. She hoped it would be enough, and she prayed the sportswriters would leave him alone.

With that, Ben and Valerie traveled together to Los Angeles for the L.A. Open. Word about Ben's surprise entry quickly leaked, and Ben and Valerie were deluged with requests for press interviews. His arrival made the front pages around the country, and crowds of admiring fans showed up to watch him play.

On the 1st hole, as Ben stooped to tee his ball, the fans rose to their feet as if in one body and began clapping. It was the strongest ovation he had ever received. Ben straightened to acknowledge their respect. He nodded once, shyly, and lowered his head to allow his eyes time to dry and to refocus on his shot.

Silence greeted Ben's swing, and then the crowd went wild. They moved with him like a shadow through his entire round, never crowding him but paying close attention to his every move. Finally, Ben was loved. Fear had pushed him to win tournaments, but it was love that would propel him to a level only one other man had ever known.

Ben played the front nine in two under par. It was a miraculous score. Standing on the 10th tee, he looked at the fans that were stampeding to get into position. He smiled to himself, wondering if any of his letter writers were in the crowd.

The back nine didn't go as well for Ben, but he finished at one over, 73 for the day. The aching tiredness in his legs had finally become a factor.

"It was awesome out there today, Val," Ben said as he sat in the bathtub soaking his legs in Epsom salts. "If it hadn't been for the fans, I would have run out of steam long before I did. It gave me energy to see them running around trying to get into place to watch me."

Valerie smiled, glad to see Ben enjoying himself. "Do you think you'll be okay tomorrow?"

"Only if my legs are. Tournaments haven't changed. Until I finish one, I'll never know how well I'll really do." Ben was busy rubbing his legs to build up the circulation in them.

"Val," Ben said, his voice lowered as if he was betraying an important confidence. "I sensed a difference in the crowds today. They were really pulling for me. And for a while, they pushed me along and helped me play. I guess my Hawk's face doesn't work anymore."

Valerie chuckled to herself when she saw Ben's smile. Just a few short months ago, he would have scowled at the idea of losing his mask.

"You know what playing in this tournament means to me, don't you?" Ben said as he continued to rub his legs.

"I know," Valerie said softly, unfolding the thick towels she had warmed on the radiator to comfort Ben's legs when he got out of the tub.

"Other than you, Val, competing means everything to me. I don't know what I would have done if I couldn't play tournament golf. I only hope my game will hold up," Ben said, finally voicing his fears aloud.

Valerie looked directly at Ben. "What separates you from the field is your brain, not your legs."

Ben's second round play was much better than his first. He shot a 69, which left him close to the lead, and he finished the day as excited as a kid.

"I don't know how I shot such a low score," Ben said as he again began his hours-long evening ritual of revitalizing his legs. "Strange things seemed to be happening out there."

"How so?" Valerie asked as she filled the bathtub with warm water.

"Well, I've never dropped so many bad putts in all my life."

Valerie's response was a smile. She knew that this was Ben's first experience with love other than her own, and the thought warmed her heart.

The start of the third round of the Los Angeles Open was delayed by Mother Nature, and talk among the pros was that the event would finish with thirty-six holes played in one day, on Sunday.

Valerie quickly grew worried. "What are you going to do?" she asked Ben. "You know your legs can't take thirty-six holes in one day." The danger of blood clots was always present.

"If they want us to play two rounds in one day, I'll just have to judge how I feel after the morning round, before teeing off again in the afternoon." Then, in unusually congenial spirits, he added, "I think I'll go downstairs and see if there are any fans who want an autograph!"

Giving up, Valerie laughed at the sight of Ben signing autographs. She didn't know who would be more surprised: Ben or the fans.

Fortunately for Ben, Saturday's round was not postponed until Sunday, just until later in the day. But, those walking with him groaned in agony as his legs slipped on the mushy ground and he slid from one side to the other. He tried using his wedge as a cane, and it helped him a bit. His legs hurt, but he refused to take time to rub them. He wanted to be treated like all the other pros.

When Ben's third round score of 69 was posted, waves of roaring fans washed over every hole of the course. Rumors circulated that Hollywood producers were at Riviera, watching Ben and talking about making a movie of his comeback.

The skies poured rain the final day, and the soggy turf again made walking very difficult. Ben's face was strained as he climbed up the hills of Hogan's Alley, inspiration from his fans pushing him. As he trudged up the 18th fairway, the gallery, soaked from sliding in the mud and rain all day, clapped as though they were one with their hero.

Ben finished with another 69 and was now in the lead. Walking off the green, he was momentarily deafened by a sudden roar of cheering from his fans. It looked as if Ben had won his first postaccident tournament with a total score of 280.

Sitting in the locker room, Toney Penna informed Ben that Sam Snead was still out on the course and had a chance to tie him. Snead needed to birdie just two of the last four holes to force a playoff.

Ben didn't think he could make it through a playoff. "I hope he birdies either three holes or none of them," he commented to Penna.

"The fans were really with you today, " Penna replied, as he ordered champagne from the waiter to celebrate Ben's return to the tour. "They tensed every time you hit a shot. I've never seen a gallery react so strongly to a golfer's play before."

"I hope I don't let them down by not being able to play tomorrow," Ben said, working on his legs to restore the circulation.

"It's not over yet," Toney countered and held up his champagne glass in a toast.

Snead did manage to birdie the last two holes and tied Ben's four-round score to force a playoff and test Ben's newfound golf game.

"Do you think your legs can go another round?" Valerie asked as Ben emerged from the locker room.

"Not in this soft ground," he said, limping to the car. "I wish Snead had won today." His voice was soft. "I really do."

"So do I," Valerie said as Ben closed her car door.

Ben was saved by Mother Nature when the playoff was rained out. And it would have to be played a week later because of Snead's schedule conflict. While Snead took off to Pebble Beach to play in the Crosby Pro-Am, Ben stayed in Los Angeles to rest. But it didn't do any good. Ben didn't have anything left in him.

Neither Snead nor Ben played particularly well in the playoff. As in all tournaments, however, there was a winner. Snead shot 71, and a tired Ben Hogan shot 76. Ben's defeat, however, gave him something almost as grand as a victory.

The night following the playoff, a dinner was held in Ben's honor. It was hosted by the two most well-known sportswriters of the day, Red Smith and Grantland Rice.

Stepping to the podium to toast Ben, Rice made one of the most quoted speeches in sports history.

> We have met here tonight to honor a man who the record books will show lost a tournament today. Well, I say he didn't lose. His legs simply were not strong enough to carry his heart around.

Ben had lost a tournament, but in doing so he had won the respect of the sportswriters at last. They would probably never love him – after all they still believed Ben had a secret he wouldn't divulge – but today he was a man who had beaten death to return to the game he loved, and for that he deserved their profound respect.

As Ben arrived at the 1950 U.S. Open at the old Merion Cricket Club outside Philadelphia, he realized he was playing a different game. Before the accident, he had played with anger – using his frustration with the sportswriters and crowds to force his concentration. Now, the concentration came more easily; he was playing with love.

On the tee, he was still a quiet, taciturn man, but the gallery's adoration of him was open, and Ben secretly reveled in the attention. The little boy who'd caddied at Glen Garden, who had been shunned and called a failure, was now accepted into the inner circle.

Ben's first round was a two-over-par 72, which put him eight strokes behind Lee Mackey. Mackey, an almost unknown pro, broke all Open records by shooting an opening 64. For the second round on Friday, Ben felt more relaxed, however, and shot a flawless 69 to move to just three strokes behind the new leader, Dutch Harrison.

Normally, this would begin talk of a Hogan victory, but the U.S. Open finished with a double round on Saturday. Whether or not Ben's legs would make the finish was the question most people were concerned with.

Because of Ben's appearance at Merion, reporters were everywhere. Ben chose his interviews carefully, as always. He met with a young sportswriter from the *Philadelphia Bulletin* on Friday evening, after finishing his routine of a rubdown and a hot bath.

"Do you find it surprising that you're still in the running after two rounds?" Harry asked.

"No. I don't," Ben replied. "I've won the Open before, and I'm here to do it again. If I thought I couldn't win on these legs, I wouldn't be here."

"Do you think your legs will be strong enough to play in the PGA later this summer?"

"As of right now, I doubt it. That tournament is six days of thirty-six-hole play each day, and I haven't found out if my legs can do one day of thirty-six holes, much less six."

"Let's hope they do," Harry commented. Then, in an off-handed way, he said, "You know, there's been a lot of talk lately about you being an enigma. After all, you came back on tour after your accident and started winning. What do you think about being called that?"

Ben snickered. "How would I feel about being called a puzzle?" He laughed again, then smiled when Harry shrugged in response. "I think I'm one of the easiest people to understand. All I want to do is play tournament golf and be the best I can." Ben smiled, seeing the reporter taking notes. "Everything I do is geared toward that end. What's the mystery?"

Ben's Saturday morning round of 72 kept him in the same position, two shots behind the leader who was now Lloyd Mangrum. Mangrum had moved up by shooting a solid 69.

Ben was in pain as he started his last round. During his lunch break, he had gone back to his hotel room and worked on his legs as best he could, but they needed rest more than anything else.

As Ben started his afternoon round, the heat of the day hit him and he was forced to slow his play to compensate for the enervating humidity. Ben felt the fans rooting for him, and he tried his best not to let anyone down.

Feeling the strain in his legs, Ben's knees locked up after his drive at the 12th tee. He almost fell but was able to grab his caddy's shoulder to steady himself.

Recovering momentarily and pushing on, Ben arrived at the 15th tee two over par for the day, two strokes better than the early leaders in the clubhouse. After he teed off, he found out that both George Fazio and Lloyd Mangrum had finished at seven-over-par totals of 287. That meant if Ben could finish at par or one over on the last four holes, he would win the Open.

Ben promptly lost a stroke to par on the 15th, one of the shortest par-fours on the course, by three-putting. His legs continued to feel the strain, but the fans cheered for him relentlessly. Ben now needed to par out to win.

He barely made his par on the 16th and then, struggling, bogeyed the long 230-yard par-three 17th quarry hole. Ben would have to par the long 458-yard par-four finishing hole to force a playoff with Fazio and Mangrum.

He stood on the 18th tee, feeling a slight breeze on his left cheek as he looked down the long fairway toward the hole. His drive split the fairway, and he slowly and painfully made his way down this last carpet of green toward his ball. His hopes for a major win, buoyed by his drive, were fueling him now.

As he walked, Ben looked at the fans running for a spot to watch his last shot to the hole. Some of them looked at him and smiled and waved. Uncharacteristically, he smiled back, and he heard one of them say, "You can do it." Ben was grateful for their encouragement.

He now stood in the middle of the fairway trying to rest his legs as Cary Middlecoff, his playing partner, hit his approach shot. Ben watched carefully as Middlecoff's ball played the wind in its approach to the green.

Arms across his chest, legs set wide for stability, Ben studied everything at his command as he took a last drag on his cigarette. It was time for him to hit a shot he had practiced thousands of times.

Ben took out his one-iron.

His eyes focused on the left middle of the green. It was nice and wide for his long shot, and it would allow him to use the wind that he felt over his left shoulder. Addressing the ball, Ben felt his body settle into place and, feeling ready, he started his backswing smoothly.

The shot started low left, just as intended, and climbed slowly up and slightly left before the wind straightened it out over the backdrop of fans ringing the green. Ben watched as it dropped onto the green and rolled to a stop about forty feet from the cup.

Ben knew what he had just done and was, for once, pleased with himself.

Walking toward the green, he realized that he felt strangely serene about the shot. He was amazed at how light his steps were. Even as he walked up the incline to the front of the green, he felt no pain.

Ben tipped his cap in thanks to his fans and, walking toward his ball, he allowed himself to look around. He had never before noticed the number of smiles in the gallery.

Ben's first putt was a touchy one. Long and slightly curved downhill on a green that was set to Open quickness, his ball glided across the fast surface. With disquieting ease, it passed the hole and stopped four feet beyond, leaving him with a tricky sidehill putt to make the playoff.

Ben had slowly walked behind the ball as it drifted toward the hole, hoping for a bird. Now, he easily walked up to it and with hardly a pause stroked his second putt.

The putt dropped.

Ben Hogan had tied for first place and was in the playoff for the 1950 U.S. Open title.

The following morning, he was intrigued by the morning newspaper's account of the day. While acknowledging that Ben had said he didn't have a secret, it later commented that Ben was playing as if he did.

As Ben readied for his practice session on the driving range, his caddy arrived with his clubs and a breathless confession. The one-iron that had helped Ben shape the extraordinary approach shot to the 18th green was now missing. His caddy had looked all over for it, but it was gone, and Ben didn't have a replacement.

"Do you want me to go get your seven-iron to bring you up to the club limit?" his caddy asked.

Ben laughed. He had removed the seven-iron to make room for the one-iron, but also because he felt no shots at Merion required a seven. "Putting the seven-iron in the bag won't create a shot for it," he remarked.

The ensuing playoff fell into Ben's hands. He missed his one-iron, and actually reached for it on the 18th fairway when he went to make his approach shot. When he remembered it was gone, he longed to feel the club in his hands once again to rifle a low shot to the green.

Finally choosing another club, he floated a four-wood onto the back of the green, a full fifty feet from the hole. Ben's putt rolled over a long hump in the green and then slowly down a flat area. It stopped close enough for a tap in for par, and Ben ended the day with a four-stroke win over Mangrum and a five-stroke win over Fazio.

Just fifteen months earlier, Ben Hogan had been in the Hotel Dieu Hospital, unable to walk, and now he was the U.S. Open champion.

Not everyone was as happy as Ben. As he and his fans discovered each other, the sportswriters continued to nag at him and, disconcertingly, other players began to tease Ben about winning.

"I hope Ben knows enough to leave some tournament trophies for the rest of us," Dutch Harrison said as he watched Ben's scores posted.

"There are a lot of guys out here who have to eat besides the Hogans," Herman Barron added with a scowl.

Ben's fellow pros, once supportive of his return to the tour, now felt Ben's success all too well. They wanted Ben to do well, but they also wanted him to stay within the pack. His eyes-ahead moving forward – and his continual topping of the leader board – made them oddly nervous.

In this atmosphere, Ben arrived at the 1951 Masters. This year, Augusta National had been altered slightly for the tournament. The tee for the 11th hole had been moved. Originally, the tee for the 11th was next to the 10th green, forcing players to hit a tricky iron tee shot to a dogleg par-four. Now, the tee was placed between trees, facing its green, creating a cathedral setting for the shot. Bobby Jones had invented Amen Corner.

As the strength ebbed from Jones's disease-striken body, his spirit entered the ground where he walked, imbuing his tournament with a special life and an electric air. Every one of the eighty-eight players felt it, and every one of them wanted all the more to win. But the Masters had its own spell for Ben, and pain in his legs or not, rain or not, Ben was there to take the Masters home.

First-round pressure was enormous that year, and scores were high. Ben shot a 70. A second round of 72 found him one stroke behind Skee Riegel, a little-known pro from Philadelphia. Tied for second with Ben was Lew Worsham, and one stroke back were top tour pros Snead, Mangrum, and Dave Douglas.

Despite the increased competition, Ben was enthused as he started his third round. He told Valerie he smelled something good in the wind, and while Valerie waited for Ben to finish his round, she shared her optimism with Bobby Jones.

"Ben thinks he's going to win this year," Valerie said happily. "When he discovered he had fans, something changed in him, Bob. He's not the man he was. He has a new purpose now, a new fire."

"Nothing would make me happier than to see Ben win this tournament," Jones said, wincing slightly as if in pain.

No one talked to Jones directly about his illness, knowing he preferred to keep news of his condition private. But Valerie was his friend, and she responded to the twinge in his voice. "Are you all right, Bob?"

"Oh, yes, I didn't mean to worry you. God knows you've been through enough lately." He had a strange, faraway look in his eyes and Valerie was startled.

"Is something bothering you?" she asked after a brief silence.

"It's nothing, Val, forgive me for disturbing you."

Looking back on the conversation in years to come, Valerie couldn't recall what made her think Jones was worried about Ben. She just knew at the time that he was, and she acted on her instincts. "Is it Ben?"

Jones sighed in mock exasperation. "I can't keep anything from you, can I? Calm down, it's nothing serious." He chuckled softly to diffuse the tension. "It's just that your mention of Ben finding out that he has fans made me think about something.

"I know that when you find your greatest love, you also encounter your greatest fear." Jones's eyes held the same faraway look in them that had frightened Valerie at the start of their conversation. "But it's nothing for us to be concerned about today," he added quickly. "Let's enjoy Ben's possible victory and leave tomorrow to tomorrow."

There was nothing more for Valerie to say, so she simply locked his words away in her heart.

Ben's third round of 70 kept him one stroke behind Riegel but still one ahead of Mangrum, while his golfing nemesis, Sam Snead, moved up.

"That's what the third round is all about," a weary Ben said to Valerie that night. "It separates the players and puts the winners in position to make a final run."

The crowd following Ben's final round was huge. They believed he was going to win his first Masters, and nothing could keep them from seeing it. Sure enough, their hero pulled away from the field, and by the end of the day, he had moved to the top position on the leader board. Ben's fellow Texan and the previous year's Master's champion, Jimmy Demaret, helped him don his first green jacket.

Oblivious to anything but his newfound fans, Ben thought his hard road was truly behind him. Choked with emotion, he said simply, "I owe it all to God and my wife, Valerie."

Chapter 11

THE ULTIMATE SECRET OF GOLF

TWO MORE WINS followed Ben's Masters victory. He had entered six tournaments in 1951 and won three of them, including another U.S. Open. The love Ben received from his fans reached the most frozen corners of his heart and gave his game a power known to only a few champions.

Then, in 1952, the love failed him and Ben stopped winning.

Rumors quickly swirled among the press corps that Ben was finished on the championship level. "It's the lingering effects of his accident," some wrote. "It's his age." "No," others argued. "It's losing the '52 Masters and the humiliation of holding the green jacket open for a healthy Sam Snead."

The antagonism between the sportswriters and Ben flared with new ferocity. They resurrected talk of Ben's hidden secret and delighted in dissecting his career.

At first Ben tried to fight it. He used every technique he had ever developed – more time on the practice range, concentration exercises, steely focus. But the harder he tried to win for his fans, the more he lost. It was a vicious circle he couldn't stop. Instead of playing to win, he found himself playing not to lose, and because of that, the inevitable happened: Ben kept losing.

At the Masters, he started the last round tied for the lead, but his final score of 79 was the highest he had ever shot at Augusta National, and he finished tied for seventh. It was a crushing slide for Ben, a man who was famous for not giving a single inch in the final round.

The U.S. Open was next, played in Texas for the first time. Ben hoped his home court advantage would lift his spirits and his game. After the first two rounds, he was in the lead with a two-stroke cushion over George Fazio. But on Open Saturday, Ben shot 74-74 to finish in third place, five strokes behind Julius Boros.

No matter what Ben did, it didn't work. He played in only two majors that year, and in those two, his final two rounds were a terrible twenty-three strokes higher than his first two rounds. Ben's game was going in the wrong direction, and that bothered him as nothing else could.

Then, MacGregor and Ben parted ways. The press needled him about this and his losses.

It didn't cheer Ben's spirits any when his fans wrote him letters of support.

Dear Ben,

My wife and I hope you won't take your recent losses too seriously. You have to remember, it's only golf.

Dear Ben,

You shouldn't worry about your new status as a past champion. You've had more than your share of wins and we'll all remember you for them.

Dear Ben,

I'm sure you've made enough money, and that's something, isn't it? All good things come to an end someday.

"These folks think losing is okay, Val. They think I should just forget about achieving my goals. What the hell is going on here?" Ben was outraged.

"In their own way, they're just trying to wish you well," Valerie encouraged.

"Well, they've missed their mark. They're giving approval to imperfection, and I won't listen to a word of it. They think having money is more important than achievement. They don't know what life is all about." Ben flicked the last of his cigarette angrily onto the back lawn where he was sitting in the fading sun. Ben Hogan wasn't dead yet, he thought.

"What do you want me to do with these letters?" Valerie asked, referring to the stack of mail in her hands.

Ben got up and began pacing. His mind went back to the days and nights spent anguishing in the hospital fighting his way back from near death.

He remembered his joy at finding out that he had fans. His work to recover had seemed so much easier with their love and support. Ben rubbed the back of his neck in thought. He had wanted to win so badly, not for himself anymore, but for his fans. He had felt like part of a team.

Now, having tried so hard to please them and having come up short, they felt heavy on his psyche, like excess luggage. Their soothing messages accepting less than victory were anything but comforting to Ben. They were contrary to everything his life had ever stood for. He was a champion. Winning – trying your best and never giving up – that's what Hogan stood for. Not losing. And certainly not the acceptance of losing.

Ben looked at the letters with disgust. The fans' approval that had meant so much to him in 1951 now felt like an albatross.

"Burn them," Ben announced with utter finality.

"Oh, Ben," Valerie pleaded. "Burn all of them? They're your fans. They mean well, after all."

Ben looked at her with pain on his face. "Then why do I feel like I've just been run over by another bus?"

Ben arrived at the 1953 Masters at one of the lowest points in his life.

"How's it coming?" Bobby Jones asked him as they sat down for drinks on the Augusta National veranda.

Ben's gloomy face gave Jones his answer.

"That bad?" Jones's voice showed his shock.

"Maybe I should give up championship golf," Ben replied. "I'm not doing myself or anyone else any good out here."

Jones didn't answer for a few moments. Ben thought it was because he agreed with him.

"Have the fans got you down, Ben?"

"The fans?" Ben slumped in his chair. "Oh, not really. For the most part, they've been great. I'm the problem. I'm letting everyone down out there. The fans, Valerie, myself, even you."

Jones scrutinized Ben's face, looking for the deeper meaning he knew was there. "In other words, you're not Ben Hogan anymore."

"Of course I'm Ben Hogan. Who else would I be?"

Jones laughed lightly. "From where I sit, it looks like you're a figment of everyone else's imagination, a guy with a burden he can't lift."

Ben was flustered and didn't know how to respond.

"Ben," Bob paused to light a cigarette, his hands shaking as he did. "I'm going to tell you something I've discussed with only one other person in the world: O.B. Keeler." Jones took a long drag, taking time to choose his words carefully. He had never expected to tell anyone the things he was about to share with Ben. But just as Jones believed his own legend as a golfer was preordained, so now did he believe it was time to rescue Ben Hogan.

He began slowly, "There's a secret to playing this game at the highest level. The spiritual level, if you will. It comes into play when you try to get past all the things that work to pull you down."

Jones's words struck a responsive cord in Ben. "That's exactly how I feel," he admitted. "Like I'm being pulled down and I can't do anything about it."

Jones smiled. "Did it happen last year when you weren't able to play well in the last round of the U.S. Open and in my own little tournament?"

Ben nodded. "It was terrible. I felt so awkward, like I didn't know what I was doing out there."

Leaning back in his chair, Jones said, "You've come a long way from those rough early days in Fort Worth."

With the reference to his youth in Fort Worth, Ben's unwanted memories surfaced, and he struggled to push them back inside. He looked out at the 13th hole in the distance, the one that had given him so much trouble the year before. It seemed to mock him.

"Even though you pretend otherwise, it would hurt like hell for you to lose the respect you've gained, wouldn't it?" Jones brought Ben back to the present in a hurry.

"You see, Ben, in the final round of a tournament, no matter how good a golfer you are, another dimension enters your game. The walls between love and fear are rubbed thin, and the love everyone has been lavishing on you suddenly becomes a stone around your neck, pulling you down.

"You're afraid of losing and, here's the bitter surprise – you're also afraid of winning. You're trapped in the middle, unable to go back and unable to move forward."

Ben leaned closer. He silently urged Jones to continue, sensing implicitly that this conversation held the key to his future as a golfer.

Jones took a long sip of his whiskey, and the ice rattled as he set his drink down. "If you lose," he said, "you know it'll all be gone. The fans, the attention, the money, the whole works. If you win, you'll climb to an even greater height. But in your heart, you also know the other players will be jealous of you, that they'll reject you.

"I've heard what the other players are saying about you,

Ben. And I know you have, too. They're happy that you're back, but you make them afraid when you step out of the pack. There is an unspoken rule that you're supposed to win only so often.

"When this dark side of love, this shadow side, sets in, Ben, you start playing with fear. Not losing everyone's love becomes more important than winning, and you play with fear from that moment on."

Jones's head was bowed in confession. Out of respect for his friend, Ben was silent. He didn't acknowledge the small tear in Jones's eye; he just let the fresh Augusta spring breeze wash over them.

Jones began again, his lips betraying a contrived smile that hid his pain. "I didn't always have this place, this course where I could simply play golf with my friends."

Jones lowered his head, and the drama of what he was about to reveal hung in the air between them. "I had to give them strokes to get them to play with me. Anytime I played, whether it was a practice round or simply a round for fun, I had to give them strokes. Here I was, playing with championship golfers, and I had to give them strokes."

Ben was amazed. "You mean to say that Armour and Hagen, and – "

"Wouldn't play with me unless I gave them strokes," Jones softly interrupted.

Ben's heart sunk. Jones had reached the pinnacle of golf, the point where he should have been loved for being a champion, and yet, incredibly, he was resented.

"When I was a small boy," Jones confessed, "I was very sickly. My mother wouldn't let me outside the house to play. Years went by, and all I could see was other children playing hide-and-seek and kick-the-can. Finally, after playing at East Lake and getting healthier, I was allowed a few friends." Bob looked at Ben, his face pale from the struggle of bringing up memories that should have been left alone to heal long ago. "Later, I couldn't risk losing my friends by continuing to beat them," Jones choked his last words out.

"And so you quit," Ben surmised.

"And so I quit."

Jones was silent for a long while before he spoke again. When he did, it was with a rising strength. "Each time you rise to the next level in golf, Ben, you risk losing the love you've already earned." Jones's face flushed with anger.

"You have no idea what it was like for me out there. Vardon and Taylor and Braid never had those crowds. Emperor Jones they called me. The emperor of golf ball striking. Would you believe it? They wanted me to win so badly they were damn well insisting on it.

"To have lost would have brought down their wrath like nothing you've ever imagined. I wasn't just a golfer to them anymore, I was a god. They collected my divots. As I walked to the next hole, there was sometimes even a fistfight for the tee. They had to install forecaddies on the course to keep the fans from stealing my balls."

"So that's why you lost so much weight every time you won a major championship?" Ben asked.

"Ben, the pressure was so enormous. Way too much for a man who really is just human after all." Jones paused, rattling the ice of his drink once again. "You were born too late, Ben. We could have had quite a time out there together."

Ben couldn't accept the finality of what Jones had told him. His mind searched for other options. "Bob, couldn't you have just blocked them out of your consciousness? Just stopped wanting their approval?"

"For me, that would have been denying reality. O.B. said at that point you start getting into real trouble." Jones drew back and sighed heavily. "If you can conquer this, Ben, and I believe you can, it will make you the greatest golfer of all time. You'll be playing at a level with which I'm not familiar."

Ben was taken aback. He had never thought of playing at Bobby Jones's level, much less beyond it.

The first day of play at the 1953 Masters found Ben in a mental daze. Everyone said he wasn't himself. He was utterly and totally preoccupied with the challenge Jones had set before him.

Ben's first round of 70 was two strokes behind the leader, Chick Harbert. Putt after putt dropped in the second round and a final score of 69 gave him a two-stroke lead.

With a great deal of effort, Ben forced all thoughts of winning and all fears of losing from his consciousness. His third round score of 66 finally separated him from the rest of the pack with a four-stroke lead. It was the best score in history for fifty-four holes on the Augusta National course.

As Ben signed his scorecard of 66, he remembered the perfect 66 Jones had scored in the 1930 British Open at Hoylake on his way to winning the Grand Slam.

"Coincidence," Ben said as he turned in his card. But the thought that what Jones had started Ben was destined to finish nagged at him.

The fourth round found a champion who now knew more about the game than anyone on the course. As he stood over his ball on the first tee, the fans roared their approval. Ben stopped and stood back. When they became quiet again, he hit his drive and was soaring with the ball, white dimples glinting over velvet fairways, dotted against a perfect blue sky.

Ben's four-round total of 274 was the lowest for any major championship in sports history. Newspapers around the country called it the finest four rounds of golf ever put together in a major tournament.

Ben was unusually silent on the drive home to Texas. Valerie thought he was mentally preparing for the U.S. Open. He wasn't. His old course, the course he had grown up on, was calling him home.

For the first time in over twenty-five years, Ben went to Glen Garden to visit the man he used to be. He shook hands with the few people who were still there from the old days and then went outside to stroll the course. It seemed smaller, shorter than he remembered, and he was flooded with memories.

Eyeing the range where he had hit balls as a youngster, Ben could see where his drives as a caddy had landed. The same distance would be no more than a seven-iron to him today.

This course, Ben thought through misting eyes, is where the real Ben Hogan was born.

As he looked out over the course, he saw trees that had continued to mature. They had changed some of the playing characteristics of the holes. For a minute, Ben considered playing a round on the course, but then realized the course's value was in his mind; it wasn't in what he could score. Glen Garden was only 6,000 yards long. Once, that length had meant a lot to him. Not now.

Ben looked at the lake where he had searched for balls and smiled, reliving the experience as if he was doing it all over again, looking for pearls. He remembered the day he was at the course trying to get a loop to take money home to his mother. It had rained, though, and no golfers turned out to play.

Ben remembered that he walked to the lake, hoping to fish out balls and sell them to the pro shop. As he arrived at the lake, he saw three older caddies already searching for balls. Ben had waited for them to finish, and then he went looking for the balls they left behind.

"Always the leftovers," Ben reminisced as he shook his head.

His visit to Glen Garden jogged something in his psyche and penetrated the wall he had built around himself. His life on tour now played out in front of him like those early films about Bobby Jones, and he sat down on the hill beside the lake to watch.

Ben remembered how hard it was for him to make the tour. He was constantly fearful of letting himself and Valerie down by losing and going broke. He had fought to be accepted by the other players and the sportswriters, even though they had belittled him by calling him the Texas Termite and Mighty Mite.

He had conquered his hook because he was afraid to make a fool of himself in front of thousands of fans. At that memory, a wave of sadness rolled over Ben, causing tears to line his eyes.

"Just when I thought I'd be accepted," Ben thought, remembering his triumphant years of 1946 and 1948, "the accident came along."

Scenes of his backbreaking recovery flooded Ben's mind. "More fear," he said to himself. "Day and night, struggling against hope that I could play golf again when everyone said I'd be lucky just to walk." He shook his head fiercely, as if to send the painful memories flying.

"My victories," he declared with a laugh. "Those sportswriters thought they knew how to write about my victories. They had no idea where my real majors were."

Wringing his hands, Ben remembered the North and South Open in Pinehurst in 1940. He had forced himself to break through the inner obstacles that had made him Mr. Runner-up. He had gone on to win in Greensboro and Asheville for three in a row, and even that wasn't good enough for the sports world.

"My name is Hogan, not Hagen," he said through clenched teeth, recalling how the sportswriters had deliberately misprinted his name to annoy him.

After the war, the sportswriters dubbed Byron Nelson "Mr. Golf." "Mr. Golf!" Ben remembered. "I showed 'em who Mr. Golf was. A new record of twenty-seven under par after my discharge – that was golf, mister!" Ben chuckled a little at his own joke.

"And Merion in 1950," Ben grinned, now speaking directly to the sportswriters. "Some of you thought that bus would do the trick, huh? No way. This game is my life."

Ben shook his head. "There's just no way I would have ever won their approval," he finally realized, an air of resignation surrounding him like the morning mist.

Ben looked out at the course again. "Only Bobby Jones understands what it's really like to be on top." The thought brought a smile to his face as he realized he had been accepted all along, by Bobby Jones of all people.

Ben's moment of joy was shortlived, however, when he also realized he had been running away from rejection his entire life and that it had impacted his game.

"My God, I've been playing their game for years," he thought. "First, I blocked them out with anger, then I played to win their love. But it was always their game. Not my own."

Ben sighed. "All this time, I thought I had gotten away with it. I should have known better."

With that, he picked himself up and slowly walked back to his car.

"From now on I'm going to play to please myself," Ben decided. "No one else."

In that moment, Ben accepted his status as an ultimate champion and gave up his fight against the shadow side of love.

As he reached the parking lot, a young caddy came over to him and asked, "Going to play today, mister?"

Ben looked down at the youngster, a thin, threadbare boy of fourteen. His eyes were a faded gray, much like Ben's own. "No thanks, son," he replied. "I just wanted to get a look at the course."

The boy looked out at the course and then back at Ben. "It's a good course. Byron Nelson and Ben Hogan used to play here."

Ben was taken aback by the mention of his name. "You don't say?"

The little boy looked at him and smiled, "If you want to play here, I'd like to be your caddy. I'll do you a good job. I've never lost a ball, and I can almost always tell you which club to use."

Ben looked down at the little boy while his mind searched for the right answer. No one should have to live with rejection, Ben thought, so he chose the softest answer he could think of. "Not right now," he murmured. "But maybe another day. I'm sure you'll do just fine."

Ben thought about the boy for a minute. They had something important in common, he thought. For both of them, their biggest challenge was still to come.

After winning the Masters, Ben easily won the Pan American Open and the Colonial Invitational at his hometown club in Fort Worth. Although Riviera already held the name, it too was being called Hogan's Alley.

In the locker room after the Colonial, Jimmy Demaret was heard to say, "Maybe we should pay Ben to skip the Colonial and Riviera next year. That might just give the rest of us a chance."

The U.S. Open was being held at Oakmont in 1953, and Ben was looking forward to playing. He had missed the 1951 PGA Championship at Oakmont because of his accident-ravaged legs, and he was curious to see if the course lived up to its reputation for controversy.

In addition to its fatiguing length of over 7,000 yards, expansive greens that invited long putts, and the most bunkers of any championship course, Oakmont furrowed grooves into its bunkers to make them more difficult. The pros had objected to Oakmont's bunkers for years, and this year the USGA forced a compromise. The bunkers around the greens would be raked smooth; the fairway bunkers would be raked in grooves.

But none of this was nearly as important to Ben as the decision to rope off the crowds for the first time in a tournament. It would help, he thought. Nevertheless, he hit his tee shots to the dead center of the fairway to distance himself further from his fans.

As Ben finished the first round, he realized his score would total 67, his lowest first-round score in any U.S. Open. "That'll mean a trip to the press tent," he thought, mentally steeling himself for the intrusion.

Walking to the press tent after handing in his card, he heard applause as his score was posted. He was three strokes ahead of the field.

Ben took a seat.

"Are you happy with your round?" a reporter up front shouted at him.

"As happy as anyone I know who shot a 67 to lead an Open," Ben answered curtly, wondering why the question was even asked.

"What do you think you're going to shoot tomorrow?" another scribe asked.

Ben twisted his face in a parody of a grin, "Somewhere between a 60 and an 80." Ben watched as the writer wrote it down, and then followed up with his own question. "Would you really print some irrelevant piece of trivia as that?"

"Can you give us a play-by-play account of your round, Mr. Hogan?"

At that, Ben stood up, brushed off his pants, and slowly trapped the reporter in a steely gaze. "If you guys ever have to report on a deaf-mute golfer, you're going to have to actually go out there and see for yourselves." For Ben, the interview was over.

A second-round 72 gave Ben a two-stroke lead over Sam Snead and George Fazio with Open Saturday coming up.

"Great position," Bobby Jones called out to Ben as they met near the back door to the locker room.

Ben held the door open for Jones as he hobbled in with his cane. They sat down in the bar area.

"All rested up for tomorrow?" Jones asked.

"That's what I'll be doing the rest of the day." He had no reason to pretend with the man who knew him better than anyone else in the world.

Jones laughed. "I remember hiding behind O.B.'s skirts after a full day at the Open. Thankfully, he cut a wide swath."

Ben took a closer look at his crippled friend. "You're really looking good. Something going on?"

Jones gave him a shy smile. "Well, I've been feeling a lot stronger since our last conversation down in Augusta.

"You relieved me of a lot of responsibility, Ben. Now the secret, and what should be done with it, lies in your hands. Not mine," Jones said as he played happily with his drink.

"Oh my God." Ben jumped out of his seat, spilling his drink.

"What's the matter?"

"I just realized something I've been denying for years," Ben said as he mopped up his drink with his handkerchief.

"I really do have a secret!"

When their laughter died down, Ben brought up the subject of the British Open. "Bob, I've decided to play in the British Open."

"What brought this on? You've never shown any interest in their Open before."

"Armour, Hutchinson, and Hagen all told me it would be good for the game, and I decided it would be good for me, also."

"Cheers," Jones toasted Ben. "But what about the PGA Championship?" That year, it was scheduled for the same weekend as the British Open.

Ben shook his head. "Well, they overlap; and I can't play both of them, can I?"

"You should go to Scotland, Ben. It's the right choice. They really need to see a great champion over there."

Ben finished the U.S. Open with scores of 73 and 71 to win by six strokes over the new perennial runner-up, Sam Snead. Ben was the first player to win both the Masters and the U.S. Open in the same year, two different times.

Arriving in Carnoustie, Scotland, for the 1953 British Open, Ben was surprised by the condition of the course. In some ways it reminded him of playing over the plains of Texas before the introduction of greenskeepers and their equipment.

Carnoustie, like most golf courses in Scotland, had no watering system other than that provided by God. That year, God must have needed the water in lands other than Scotland because it was very dry, and the course was an ugly brown.

As Ben looked out upon Carnoustie for the first time,

he realized all of the challenges that would await him, and a tiny flame grew brighter in his heart. He loved the challenges of the game and silently wondered to himself why he had never considered playing in Scotland before.

In the States, bunkers were placed in certain places for prearranged reasons, but in Scotland, bunkers were thought to have been placed by burrowing animals, and they could appear anywhere, making local knowledge a bigger factor in the game.

The Scottish game also demanded different kinds of shots to keep the ball below the influence of the ever-present wind. Approach shots to the greens needed to bump and run, because the greens were so slick they could scarcely hold anything with a trajectory sharper than an eight-iron.

Ben was amused by everything he saw, but it was the local people of Scotland who really intrigued him. As he practiced, whole families traipsed after him, children in strollers, grandmothers in aprons. As he practiced putting, many of the villagers spread out a picnic lunch to further enjoy their day.

It was truly a public course. Life revolved around the course, and life happened on the course.

What Ben loved about the Scottish fans most of all, though, was how well they seemed to know the game. They cheered only the best shots and gave the players enough room to perform without interference. They made room for him to walk through to the next tee, never asking for an autograph, never interrupting his concentration.

Ben's opening round of 73 left him three strokes behind the heir to the Champion Spark Plug fortune, Frank

Stranahan, an American amateur who made an annual trip to Europe to play in the British Open.

In the second round, Ben shot a 71, which left him two strokes back of the lead. Finding Ben in the clubhouse after play, Valerie said, "Have you heard that a lot of American radio stations are carrying the broadcast rights for the Open because you're here?"

Ben gazed Valerie's way, an absentminded look on his face. "Did I mention that after we finish here the best way back to the States seems to run through Paris?"

"Oh, Ben, that's wonderful! Do you mean it?"

He nodded and smiled.

"I'd love to see Paris. It might just make following you from sandtrap to sandtrap worthwhile for the next two days."

Ben was shocked. "They're bunkers, not sandtraps!"

"Yes, and there are other ways home than through Paris, too."

Ben's third round of 70 moved him into a tie for the lead with Roberto DiVicenzo. Their lead was a slim one, however, as Dai Rees, Peter Thomson, and Tony Cerda were all one stroke back.

Lunching with his caddy, Ben readied himself for the fourth round, which would be played that afternoon. He intended to play conservatively, unless scoring dictated a different plan.

The fourth round unfolded as Ben expected. In approaching the par-four 5th hole, he lined up his seven-iron, and with utmost inner quiet, he hit a shot so perfectly, he didn't watch its flight.

Ben's caddy watched the ball and was shocked to realize Ben had walked on before it landed. "Ye dinna watch the ball, sir," his caddy lilted, a slight question hanging in the air.

Ben was busy getting his putter out for his next stroke.

The caddy cleared his throat and repeated himself, this time a little louder. "Ye dinna watch the ball."

Ben turned back and cast his steely gaze upon his caddy. "That's because they go exactly where I want them to go."

On the 18th hole, Ben discovered he had a three-stroke lead as he made his final birdie of the day. As he holed his putt, the fans stood to show their respect. A quiet clapping moved through the crowd. They were professional in their awe to the end.

Ben's fourth-round score of 68 not only won him the tournament and the cherished Claret Jug, it set a new record for Carnoustie and for the British Open.

Everyone knew Ben had accomplished the impossible. In a single year, he had won the Masters, the U.S. Open, and now the British Open.

As Ben stood clasping the old Claret Jug, he realized Scotland was a place that would have accepted him as he was. It was a land of gracious people who loved golf the way he and Bobby Jones did, who made golf part of their daily lives and respected others who did the same. Yes, here was a place his soul would have called home. But he was already the "Wee Ice Mon," as the Scottish press had nicknamed him, and now he couldn't go back.

Chapter 12

THE REAL HOGAN EMERGES

BEN LEANED BACK in his easy chair, nearly forty-three years after his spectacular win at Carnoustie. The triangular orange slices that he had cut earlier still rested in their small ceramic bowl on the armrest of his lounger. He laughed when he noticed them. Oranges. Instead of reminding him of his years of failure, though, the oranges now seemed to recall his steely determination and the success that resulted from it.

The rush of memories, so uncharacteristic of Ben Hogan, strangely, did not disturb him any longer. He had one last obstacle to overcome, and he realized that he had avoided it as long as he could.

He did have a secret, and he needed to decide what to do with it.

The garage door quietly clicked shut. Valerie, the non-playing partner of the Hogan team, was home from her shopping trip.

She quietly walked through the kitchen. Life was peaceful for her and Ben now, no more traveling, no more rushing to meet his tournament schedule. She rather liked being a housewife, settled in one place, even if it had come to her so late in life.

She called out to Ben and was surprised when she didn't receive a response. She had seen his car in the garage.

"Ben?" Valerie called out a second time. "Where are you?"

"I'm in here," Ben said softly from his chair in the den. On her way to see him, Valerie saw the bowl of cut oranges sitting on the armrest of Ben's chair. It was an odd sight, so unlike Ben to leave food uneaten.

"Why didn't you answer me right away? Is anything wrong?" The look on Ben's face told her there was. It was a look she hadn't seen in many years. The gray of his eyes was dark and piecing.

Frightened now, Valerie quickly said, "Ben Hogan, answer me. Are you all right?"

Ben's face slowly broke into a twisted smile as he turned to look at her.

"Ben, what is going on? Talk to me."

"You won't believe what happened today," he said, rubbing his legs. "Look what showed back up?" He handed Valerie the one-iron, which had not left his side all day, and told her the story of the club's reappearance.

"Is this the one you lost at Merion?" she asked.

"None other," Ben said as he took the club from Valerie. "It found its way back to me today, after all these years." Ben's voice trailed to a whisper and Valerie knew there was more to the story than a rediscovered one-iron. She waited for him to explain.

"It may have come as a reminder, Val." Ben's voice had

an unearthly quality to it. It was soft and dreamy, already part of another world, and it heightened Valerie's fear.

"A reminder of what?" Valerie coaxed, as she bent over to hold Ben's hand.

"A reminder that I still haven't done anything about the secret. If I die with it, Val, it may take years for someone else to discover it."

"Oh, Ben, I don't like to hear you talk this way. You'll be here for a long time yet."

"We've faced this subject before, you and I. The accident wasn't that long ago," he said, his eyes warm and liquid now, more brown than gray, fixed on Valerie and capturing her mind and her heart as he had always done.

"Yes, I know," she answered, quickly looking away. "But this is different. You sound as if you're planning something."

Ben was quiet, and Valerie knew he had retreated into the focused corners of his mind to resolve a problem.

"Really, Ben, what can you do with the secret at this stage in your life?" she added, hoping to persuade Ben to drop the subject. To divulge the secret now would expose Ben to enormous media scrutiny, and might even make him look like a fool. "You've done enough for the game of golf."

"Have I?" Ben said as he stared out the window, seeing everything and seeing nothing. His faraway voice soon broke the silence, and Valerie realized Ben would not be dissuaded.

"I thought someone would step out in front by now. There's been no one since Nicklaus and Palmer." Ben lit a cigarette, thoroughly lost in his musings and relaxing with them.

"Remember when we were growing up? They said there would never be another Harry Vardon. Then along came Bobby Jones." Ben laughed, breaking the tension. "He ruined their calculations, didn't he?"

Ben took a long drag on his cigarette, and as he did so his legendary anger flamed along with the ashes. "I'll bet most of the guys on tour today don't even know the name of the first guy to win six British Opens or the guy who won four in a row.

"They don't want to learn from the past, Val, There's too much money out there, and it's obscuring their vision." Ben had reached the core of the problem. He stubbed out his cigarette and reached for another one, but held off lighting it. His thoughts were tumbling out and wanted no interference from his hands.

"Remember how closely we watched Tom Watson, thinking he would finally match Vardon? We were the only ones who saw what was happening. He was a different man when he played the British. Why didn't the world recognize it?"

Ben leaned back in his chair and finally lit his cigarette. "I wish Bob was here, Val. He'd know what to do."

It was time for Valerie to give Ben the support he had come to rely upon. "I know how much you've been pulling for another golfer to come along and beat your record. Even if the world doesn't know it, I do." She rose from her seat and kissed Ben's forehead as she went into the kitchen to pour coffee.

When she returned, she realized Ben was still talking. He hadn't noticed her absence. ". . . a hot new player will come along and I can predict the greeting he'll receive from the tour. He'll say, 'I'm gonna win my first pro event.' And the pack will say, 'You'll learn, kid, you'll learn.' No one understands the force that controls the pack."

Ben shook his head, wondering how to save the game he loved so much. Rubbing his legs again, he got up and paced the room, leaving Valerie to her coffee.

Scratching his head, Ben finally noticed Valerie's presence. He looked at her and calmly announced his decision. "Val, I guess I'm going to have to come out in the open again."

Valerie winced with pain. She suspected Ben would decide to disclose the secret, but she was not prepared for the finality of his words. "But, Ben," she argued one last time, "you gave everyone your secrets when you wrote *Power Golf* and *The Modern Fundamentals*. No one believed you. What will be different this time?"

"I've got an idea," Ben said with a wry smile on his face. "This time, I think I'll have the last word."

The next morning, Valerie woke early to find that Ben had already left for his office and Shady Oaks. Making herself a cup of coffee, she settled into Ben's favorite chair in the den to think. Sun streamed in through the trees, capturing the window and her chair in a burst of sunbeams. The corner of her eye caught an illuminated piece of paper on the desk to the right of the window.

Thinking Ben had left her a note, she rose to read it. There she found a letter to the USGA instructing it to send the enclosed letter to its members "upon my death." She winced at the mention of Ben's death and then smiled at his cleverness. "So that's how he's going to have the last word." She laughed as she read the letter.

BEN HOGAN'S SECRET

Dear USGA Member,

I'm sure receiving a letter from me will come as a surprise to you. I lived my life in a rather private way and never felt the need to speak out. But over the last few years, a change has come over the way golf is played. This change has nothing to do with better clubs or better balls. The game simply no longer produces champions and, although it is hard for me to believe, I seem to be the only one who knows why.

A reporter once wrote that "Hogan defined golf." While that may have been true in some years, like many reporters, he didn't grasp the essence of the game he covered. Golf defined me. It was my life. Every day I played golf – whether it was a full round or a day of practice – was a special blessing to me. I couldn't wait for the sun to come up because I knew golf would be part of my day. I played golf because I enjoyed it and because it gave me opportunities I couldn't find anywhere else.

Some of you may know something about my background. Most of you don't. My family wasn't rich. They were poor. I didn't practice at country clubs. I used any course and any field I could walk to. I didn't have sponsors to help me stay on tour. If I didn't win, I had to quit because I didn't have enough money to continue. I worked for everything I achieved. In a way, I had more advantages than the golfers on tour today because I knew what it took to win. They don't.

Haven't you wondered about this? Don't you want to know why our professional golfers win a major tournament or two and then retreat into obscurity? Don't you wonder why they win two or three tournaments in one year and are never heard from again? Of course you do.

You've heard the excuses just as I have. There's more competition on today's tour. Baloney! If Harry Vardon or Bobby Jones came back today and played golf on better courses with today's better equipment, they would dominate the game just like they did in their time. Why is this?

There's too much talk today among professional players about comfort zones, about companionship being more important than winning. This is utter nonsense. There is only one reason to play the game of golf. To win. Not to win against an opponent. To win against yourself, to overcome your own obstacles, to find out what kind of man or woman you are.

Obstacles are not there to tell you to quit or to help you find your comfort zones. Obstacles are there to give you determination, for without determination, you'll never be a winner.

When you decide to win, a lot of people will try to hold you back. They'll be jealous of you and enjoy watching you stumble. They may even laugh at you. They'll say you have a lot to learn, that you're not a champion until you attend awards dinners, sign autographs, and chew up your practice time playing in tournaments with paid appearance fees. Don't listen to them.

The next great champion will not come out of the pack. He (or she) will not play by anyone else's rules. He'll be controversial, and he'll change the game.

When you decide to win, don't be surprised if you try to hold yourself back, too. It won't just be others who will be in your way. At each step of the way, you'll be reluctant to risk what you've already gained. You'll be tempted to join the pack, to do things their way, so that the criticism will stop. Don't give in.

I wasn't born a champion. Golf made me a champion. Without golf, I would still be digging a meager living out of the Texas hills.

By now, it should be clear to you that I want you to become a champion. Why? Because the world needs champions to show others the way. Should it be golf? I can't answer that for you, but I can give you the formula I've found that will make you a champion in whatever you do.

1. Find something you love.
2. Give your whole heart to it.
3. Don't let anyone or anything come between you and your goal.

The last step was the most excruciating for me. I had to mount a twenty-four hour effort every day to achieve it. As you get onto your path, you'll find out just as I did how hard the last step is. But the rewards will more than offset the effort.

I wish you a good game and a good life.

Golfingly yours,
Ben Hogan

POSITIVELY IMPACT YOUR CLUB

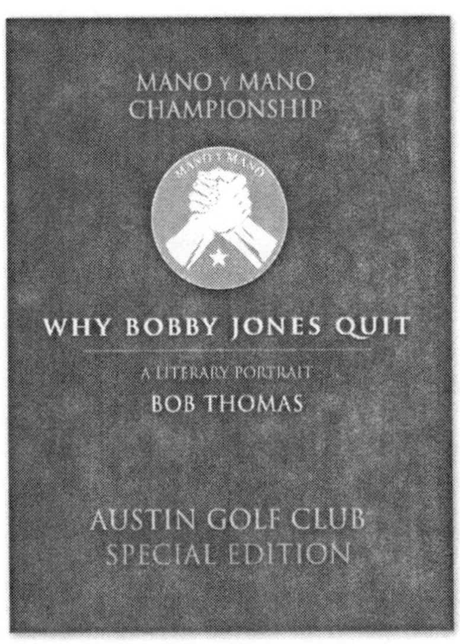

Give out a Tournament Edition of this book at your next tournament

Prestigious hardback editions of my books are available with your club's name on the cover, the logo on the inside flap, and a foreword from the club's pro (which we write for the pro) as the first page of the book.

Here's the Tournament edition I did of my Bobby Jones book for the Austin Golf Club last year, used in the Mano y Mano Championship.

HERE'S WHAT YOUR CLUB CAN DO WITH A TOURNAMENT EDITION:

- As goodie bags or tee gifts
- At corporate tournaments – to wow corporate executives
- To acknowledge a senior member's time in the game
- As a special banquet table gift for special occasions
- To tie your tournament in with a great player – like Hogan or Jones
- As a new member gift
- As a marketing piece
- To impress someone who can help your club

GIVE ME A CALL:

Bob Thomas (910) 368-1884